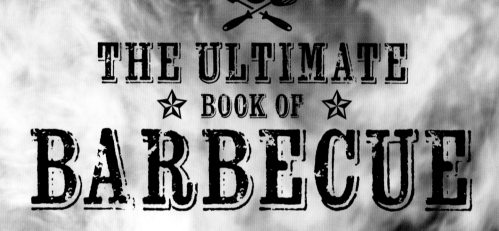

THE ULTIMATE
☆ BOOK OF ☆
BARBECUE

THE ULTIMATE
☆ BOOK OF ☆
BARBECUE

A DELICIOUS COLLECTION OF BARBECUE RECIPES

LOVE FOOD™

This edition published by Parragon Books Ltd in 2015 and distributed by

Parragon Inc.
440 Park Avenue South, 13th Floor
New York, NY 10016
www.parragon.com/lovefood

LOVE FOOD is an imprint of Parragon Books Ltd

ISBN 978-1-4723-7367-0

Printed in China

New recipes and home economy by Lincoln Jefferson
New photography by Mike Cooper
New text by Robin Donovan
Edited and project managed by Cheryl Warner
Designed by Lexi L'Esteve
Illustrations by Scott Rhodes, courtesy of The Bright Agency

Notes for the Reader
This book uses standard kitchen measuring spoons and cups. All spoon and cup
measurements are level unless otherwise indicated. Unless otherwise stated, milk is
assumed to be whole, eggs are large, individual vegetables are medium, and pepper
is freshly ground black pepper. Unless otherwise stated, all root vegetables should
be peeled prior to using.

Garnishes, decorations, and serving suggestions are all optional and not
necessarily included in the recipe ingredients or method. The times given are only
an approximate guide. Preparation times differ according to the techniques used by
different people and the cooking times may also vary from those given. Optional
ingredients, variations, or serving suggestions have not been included in the
time calculations.

Contents

Bring On The Barbecue!

Food and fire combine to create one of the best things in life—barbecue. Add a patio full of friends, a pair of barbecue tongs in one hand, and a cold beer in the other, and it doesn't get much better. Grilling food—meat, veggies, or even fish or fruit—over hot coals brings a deep, primal sense of satisfaction and pleasure. And nothing brings out the natural flavors of meat and vegetables in the way cooking them on the grill does—whether using a high-heat, fast-grilling method, low-and-slow cooking, or smoking. Not to mention, barbecuing is fast, delicious, and easy to clean up.

A GRILL FOR EVERY PERSON, PLACE, AND OCCASION

The array of barbecue grills on the market these days is mind-boggling—gas, charcoal, or electric, gigantic or small enough to carry to the beach. Whether you opt for a backyard gas grill, a balcony-size electric grill, or an on-the-road charcoal grill is a personal choice and depends on your barbecue priorities. Whether you want intense smoky flavor or a system that will let you cook a delicious and healthy meal any place, any time, there is a grill that is just right for you.

CHARCOAL, WOOD, OR GAS?

If it's smoky, chargrilled flavor that draws you to barbecuing, a charcoal or wood grill is your best bet. If, however, convenience, speed, and easy cleanup are most important to you, a gas grill cannot be beaten. The recipes in this book are designed to be cooked on any of these types of grills, so whichever you decide to use, it will be suitable for these recipes.

CHARCOAL GRILLS AND KETTLES

Charcoal grills come in many shapes and sizes. The kettle grill is the standard-style grill. Round with a deep bowl, a kettle grill has a grate in the bottom that the charcoal sits on and, above that, a grill where the food is cooked. Simple and functional, this type of grill is the perfect solution for the frequent or occasional barbecue cook because it is sturdy, inexpensive, and versatile. You can use a kettle grill for high-heat grilling, slower indirect cooking (what's known in barbecue circles as true barbecuing), and even as a smoker.

Charcoal grills also come in small, portable tabletop versions, as well as large rectangular versions. Whichever you choose, look for one with sturdy legs and adjustable vents, which will give you the ability to control the heat of your fire.

6

Charcoal briquettes, which are manufactured from wood by-products, are easy to find (they're available in most supermarkets), inexpensive, and easy to transport, making them perhaps more convenient than wood. Easy-light varieties make using charcoal more convenient than ever—with these, you won't even need lighter fluid.

Lump charcoal, on the other hand, is a more natural form of charcoal. To make it, logs are burned in an oxygen-free environment. They are generally made without a lot of additives (meaning you won't get even a hint of lighter fluid's flavor in your food), leading purists to choose them over briquettes.

WOOD-FIRED GRILLS

Charcoal grills can also be used as wood-fired grills. The appeal of grilling over wood is that it adds flavor and, many think, is less polluting than charcoal. You can buy bags of wood chips and/or large hunks of various types of wood. Wood can be a lot more finicky than charcoal to cook with, because you have to contend with many different factors, such as how dry the wood is or how big the pieces are—both of which affect how hot or fast they burn, how much smoke they put out, and what flavor they impart (for more on types of wood, see page 212).

Pellet grills use small pellets made by compressing sawdust instead of whole pieces of wood. These pellets come in a variety of "flavors" and burn cleanly and quickly to a fine ash. The small size and easy-to-control burn of the pellets means that these types of grills offer the best of both worlds. You get ease of use and convenience similar to a gas grill with the added smoky flavor of a hardwood grilling.

GAS GRILLS

Gas grills are ideal for people who want to be able to cook a meal quickly and enjoy minimal cleanup. The biggest benefits of gas grills are that they heat up in minutes with the turn of a dial, have easily controlled heat, are easy to clean, and are less polluting than charcoal. The downside of gas grills is that they don't work well for smoking and don't impart that delectable smoky, chargrilled flavor. Some barbecue purists turn their noses up at gas grills, but they are practical.

Like charcoal grills, gas grills come in a wide range of styles from small portable models to gigantic backyard behemoths capable of grilling large quantities for a crowd. Whichever size of gas grill you choose, go for the best quality you can afford.

Gas grills with multiple burners are key to being able to control your heat and have versatility in your cooking abilities. Having two burners lets you use both direct and indirect heat. Having three or more burners gives you even more heat control. Angled metal plates over the burners keep the heat evenly dispersed and prevent flare-ups. If you want to combine the convenience of a gas grill with the smoky flavor-imparting abilities of a charcoal one, look for a gas grill with lava rocks. These are hard to find and more expensive, but if you're handy, you might be able to rig a standard gas grill to get the same effect.

ELECTRIC GRILLS

A new breed of outdoor electric grills has hit the market in recent years, opening up barbecuing possibilities for those with no outdoor space except a small balcony or patio. While they don't have the power of either charcoal or gas, if it's your only choice, it will certainly do.

SMOKERS

To make delicious smoked meats, all you really need is a basic charcoal grill, but if you want to impress your friends, some additional equipment is needed. Fortunately, there are plenty of stand-alone smokers and smoker attachments to choose from. With these, you can produce fantastic smoked foods without having to hover over the machine all day, checking and adjusting the temperature, adding wood chips, or basting the meat. A good smoker or smoker attachment lets you set it and forget it and still put a great tasting meal on the table at the end of the day. You can also adapt charcoal, gas, and electric grills for smoking (see right).

SMOKER ATTACHMENTS

The simplest way to equip yourself for barbecue smoking is a smoker attachment that extends the abilities of the grill you already have. If you've got a kettle grill, for example, you can probably buy an inexpensive attachment that will turn it into a stand-alone smoker.

Many gas grills can be upgraded with a smoker box attachment. This is a heavy, vented metal container that holds wood chips and enables you to smoke foods on the gas grill you already have.

VERTICAL GAS SMOKERS

Vertical gas smokers are less versatile, because they can do only one thing, but they do a great job of smoking meats and are easy to use.

DRUM-, BULLET-, OR CONE-SHAPE SMOKERS

Charcoal-fired drum, bullet, and cone- or egg-shape smokers are more expensive, but they create great smoky flavor and are easy to keep at a low temperature, which is essential if you want smoky flavor without drying out your food.

If you're serious about smoking, pellet smokers—grills fueled by burning small pellets of compressed hardwood sawdust—are a good choice. They are easy to use, hold a temperature well, and create a distinctive, yet still delicate, smoky flavor.

Get Things Cookin'

No matter what type of grill you choose and whether you're using gas, wood, or charcoal, grilling is a fun and easy way to make tasty meals. Using three main methods—direct-heat cooking, indirect-heat cooking, and smoking—you can use your grill to make a head-spinning, mouth-watering array of foods.

DIRECT-HEAT COOKING

Direct-heat grilling refers to the intense, high-heat grilling most people use to sear a steak, quick-cook burgers to a beautiful medium-rare, or grill salmon just until it has those nice black grill marks and is cooked through but still moist and tender in the middle. Use direct-heat cooking when you want to sear the food quickly, give it a nice charred flavor, and caramelize the outside without drying out the center. Ideally, foods that you intend to cook over direct heat should be seasoned with dry spices or spice rubs. They can also be marinated, but if you use a glaze that contains sugar, wait until the end of the cooking time to brush it on to prevent the sugar from burning.

The direct-heat grilling method is ideal for steaks, chops, burgers, fish, shellfish, chicken, sausages, and vegetables.

In direct cooking, the food is cooked directly above the heat source. With charcoal, this means simply placing the pile of hot coals under the area where you plan to cook. You can even use one side of the grill for direct-heat cooking by pushing all of the coals to that side, but leaving the other side of the grill open for indirect cooking. To use direct-heat cooking on a gas, wood-fired, or electric grill, simply place the food directly over the burners or heat source.

No matter how much of the grill you intend to use for direct-heat cooking, it's a good idea to oil the grill rack to keep your food from sticking. To oil the grill rack, soak a folded paper towel with oil and then use a grill-cleaning brush or long-handle barbecue tongs to rub the oil-soaked towel over the rack until it is well-coated with oil. Note that the oil will smoke a little as you do this, but this is perfectly fine.

Direct-heat cooking, then, is accomplished by placing the food onto the oiled grill rack directly over hot coals or hot burners, cooking for a few minutes on one side, then turning and cooking for a few minutes on the other.

INDIRECT-HEAT COOKING

Indirect-heat cooking is a "low-and-slow" method of grilling, where you place the food on a hot grill rack but not directly on top of the heat source. Additionally, the grill's cover is kept closed during cooking to keep the heat in. When using charcoal or wood, you simply push the hot coals or wood to the side to make a space on the grill that does not have the heat directly under it. On a gas grill, you can accomplish the same thing by heating up the grill with all of the burners on and then turning off one or two of them to make a space where you can cook the food without it being directly over the heat source.

This method is best for longer-cooking cuts of meat, such as roasts, whole chickens or turkeys, and other slow-cooking foods.

As in direct-heat cooking, it's a good idea to oil the grill rack to keep your food from sticking. First heat the grill, then move the coals away from your cooking area or turn off the burners in that area, soak a folded paper towel with oil, and then use a grill-cleaning brush or long-handle barbecue tongs to rub the oil-soaked towel over the grill rack until it is well-coated with oil.

SMOKING

Smoking is a general term for using heat and smoke (from wood and/or charcoal) to cook food. Food is placed onto the grill, which is then closed and filled with heat and smoke (see pages 8 and 9 for smokers and smoker attachments). This process cooks and flavors the meat simultaneously. Smoking is generally done at lower temperatures, which allows for the foods to have time to absorb the smoky flavor while still cooking at a steady enough temperature to safely keep bacteria at bay.

Turn Up the Heat

Here is how to start and heat up various types of barbecue.

COOKING WITH WOOD

To build a wood fire, follow these simple steps.

1. Make a small pile of twigs and paper scraps on the charcoal grate of your grill.

2. Construct a "tepee" of small sticks Over the twig pile, balancing the sticks against each other so that they stand up with room for air to circulate underneath.

3. Light a match and hold it to the twigs and paper scraps until they ignite. Light the sticks in several places.

4. When the sticks catch fire, begin adding increasingly large pieces, waiting for them to catch fire before adding more.

5. Once you've got a good strong fire, begin adding the larger logs, being sure to lean them against each other, always leaving room for air to circulate underneath.

6. Once the fire is blazing, let it go for about 40 minutes for a really hot heat source. Once the logs are glowing and hot, use a poker, barbecue tongs, or a long stick to distribute them as you want under the grill.

CHARCOAL BRIQUETTES IN A CHIMNEY STARTER

To light charcoal briquettes, a chimney starter—a cylindrical device that lets you light your briquettes quickly and without lighter fluid—is highly recommended. If you've got one, put it on the charcoal grate of your barbecue, fill the bottom section with wadded-up newspaper, and fill the top section with charcoal briquettes. Using a match or lighter, ignite the newspaper. Once the coals catch fire, give them about 20 minutes to get hot. Once all of the briquettes are coated with white ash, they are ready to spread out. Carefully tip them out of the chimney onto the charcoal grate and spread the coals out, using a long stick or barbecue tongs.

CHARCOAL BRIQUETTES WITH LIGHTER FLUID

If using regular, untreated charcoal briquettes without a chimney starter, make a pile of the briquettes on the charcoal grate of your grill. Douse the pile with lighter fluid and give it a few minutes to soak in (while you wait, put the cap securely onto the lighter fluid container and place it at a safe distance from the grill). Using a match or lighter, light the briquettes in several places and let them burn for 30—40 minutes, until they are all glowing red and covered with white ash. Once they're hot enough, spread them out for an even cooking area, using barbecue tongs or a long stick.

EASY-LIGHT BRIQUETTES

Because easy-light briquettes are pretreated with lighter fluid, they are convenient and easy to use. Simply pile pretreated briquettes on the charcoal grate of your grill and light with a match. The briquettes will be ready for grilling when they are glowing and mostly covered with white ash, which will take 30—40 minutes. Once they're hot enough, spread them out for an even cooking area, using barbecue tongs or a long stick.

LIGHTING A GAS GRILL

The most important thing to remember when lighting a gas grill is to do so with the lid open. Otherwise there is the potential for gas to build up inside. In this case, sudden ignition could lead to a dangerous explosion. Beyond that, every gas grill is a little different, so simply follow the manufacturers' instructions for lighting and preheating.

LOW, MEDIUM, AND HOT HEAT

What has to be one of the most important elements of a good barbecue is to get the grill heat just right. If you don't, then no matter how good your recipe or ingredients are, your results could be disastrous. This simple technique will prevent culinary mishaps caused by a too hot or too cool fire.

To roughly determine how hot a fire is, place your hand just above the grill and count seconds (for example "one Mississippi, two Mississippi ..."). When a fire reaches hot heat(450°F—550°F), you'll need to pull your hand away in 1—2 seconds. With a medium-heat fire (325°F—350°F), you'll be able to keep your hand there for about 3 seconds. With a low-heat fire (225°F—250°F), you can keep your hand there for 4—5 seconds.

In this book, the recipes state to preheat to certain temperatures. These temperatures are:

Low: 225°F–250°F
Medium-low: 260°F–300°F
Medium: 325°F–350°F
Medium-hot: 375°F–425°F
Hot: 450°F–550°F

Please check the grill temperature is correct, using a thermometer before starting to cook, for absolute accuracy.

BASIC TOOLS YOU NEED

Once you've got your grill and fuel worked out, there are just a few tools you'll need to invest in. You can find plenty of fun barbecue tools that may enhance your barbecue, but here is a list of absolutely essential barbecue tools (for more on barbecue tools, see page 148):

TONGS

A nice sturdy pair of long-handle tongs is essential for maneuvering hot food around the grill. Stainless steel, spring-loaded tongs are good for durability and ease of use. A second pair of tongs reserved for moving around hot coals and other nonfood items is also extremely handy.

SKEWERS

There are two main choices to consider when choosing skewers. The first is disposable bamboo skewers. The benefits of these are that they are inexpensive and don't need to be cleaned. Of course, their disposability can also be seen as a negative. Another downside is that they need to be presoaked in water for 30 minutes before placing on a hot grill to prevent them from burning.

The second choice is long metal skewers with a flat-blade design (as opposed to cylindrical metal sticks). The blade design prevents food from turning on the skewer when you attempt to turn the skewers over on the grill. The fact that these are reusable is a benefit; however, of course that means they must be cleaned after each use. Look for metal skewers with heat-resistant handles, otherwise prepare to use oven mitts to avoid burning yourself on the hot metal when you turn the skewers over on the grill.

BASTER

A long-handle, natural fiber brush (stay away from anything that might melt at high heat) or a mop-style baster is useful for basting meats with marinade as they cook.

WIRE BRUSH

A long-handle wire brush is essential for cleaning the grill.

THERMOMETER

This is especially helpful for checking that the grill has reached the desired temperature before cooking.

MEAT THERMOMETER

An instant-read meat thermometer is extremely useful for checking the temperature of meat to be sure it is done. This is particularly important with large cuts of meat, such as roasts or whole chickens or turkeys.

Is It Done Yet?

Now that you've invested in a handsome grill, outfitted yourself with essential barbecue tools, and are ready to get cooking, let's just take a minute to talk about safety. Cooking food until it is properly done is crucial for avoiding food poisoning, but knowing when food reaches this point can be a tricky business. There are a couple of different ways to test meat for doneness.

WHOLE OR PIECES OF CHICKEN OR TURKEY

To check a whole chicken for doneness, insert the tip of a sharp knife into the thickest part of one of the thighs. If it's done, the juices should run clear. Wiggling a drumstick is another method. If the chicken is done, the drumstick will turn easily and feel loose. For a separate piece, cut through the thickest part of the meat to be sure there is no sign of pink.

BURGERS, SAUSAGES, AND PORK

These should be cooked until the center is no longer pink and the juices run clear.

FISH

It's relatively easy to tell when fish is cooked through. Simply press on the fish at its thickest point. If it is done, the flesh will flake easily.

SHRIMP

Cook until they are fully opaque and turn pink.

OYSTERS, MUSSELS, AND CLAMS

Discard any with open shells before cooking. Cook until the shells open fully and discard any with shells that do not open after sufficient cooking.

THERMOMETER METHOD

To be really safe, opt for the thermometer method, which is more essential when cooking large cuts of meat, such as roasts, legs of lamb, or whole turkeys. Use a digital, instant-read thermometer inserted at the thickest part of the meat (be sure it is not touching bone) and refer to this chart:

TYPE OF MEAT	MINIMUM	MEDIUM-RARE	MEDIUM	WELL-DONE
BEEF	145°F	145°F	160°F	170°F (OR HIGHER)
LAMB	145°F	145°F	160°F	170°F (OR HIGHER)
PORK	145°F	N/A	160°F	170°F (OR HIGHER)
GROUND MEAT	160°F	160°F	165°F	170°F (OR HIGHER)
POULTRY	165°F	N/A	165°F	170°F (OR HIGHER)

Please also check current government guidelines for the latest information on cooking temperatures.

GENERAL FOOD SAFETY

Use common sense and basic food safety rules when it comes to preparing and storing food outside. For instance, always wash your hands before handling food, whether you are having a barbecue in your backyard or cooking in the kitchen.

Bacteria can grow and multiply in any type of food, and they thrive at temperatures between 40°F and 140°F. Keep food—especially meat, poultry, and seafood—in the refrigerator or a cooler (below 40°F) until ready to prepare for cooking.

Thoroughly thaw frozen meat, poultry, or fish before grilling to be sure of even cooking.

Always keep raw meat, fish, or poultry apart from cooked foods. If you use utensils or dishes to handle raw meat, wash them thoroughly before using them for cooked food.

SAFE GRILLING

Fire is a dangerous beast and every time you light up your grill, you are welcoming it into your yard. There's no reason your family can't live peacefully with it, but a few precautions are necessary.

1.   Have a fire extinguisher nearby and know how to use it.
2.   Don't put your grill or smoker too close to buildings, trees, foliage, or other flammable materials. Check the instructions for minimum distances.
3.   Make sure that one person is in charge of watching the grill at all times.
4.   Minimize flare-ups by keeping your grill or smoker clean. Clean grates completely with a wire brush, empty ashes, and brush all surfaces clean after every use.
5.   Inspect any grill, especially a gas grill, regularly to make sure there are no blockages or other problems that could cause a dangerous situation.
6.   If using charcoal with lighter fluid, be extremely careful. Never add lighter fluid to burning coals and, of course, keep the container of lighter fluid tightly sealed and far away from the fire.
7.   Keep children a good distance from hot surfaces and any equipment or fuel.

GET GRILLIN'

Once you've got your grill, your tools, and your methods worked out, it's time to fire up that bad boy and start cooking. The recipes here are designed to be easy to use, but they never skimp on flavor. So what are you waiting for? Fire up that 'cue, crack a cold one, and get cooking!

Chapter 1
RUBS & MARINADES

How to Use Spice Rubs, Marinades, and Glazes

Spice rubs, marinades, and glazes add complex flavor to your grilled foods. Each functions slightly differently and their methods of use vary as well.

SPICE RUBS

Dry rubs are mixtures of dried spices and aromatics that are slathered onto meat before cooking. Wet rubs contain oil or other liquid ingredients. While both types permeate the meat with intense flavor, dry rubs do so without adding moisture to the cooking equation, which is critical if you want crisply seared or charred meat.

A good rub combines the four primary flavors: sweet, salty, sour, and bitter. Start with the basics—salt and sugar—and from there you can add any combination of aromatics, such as fresh or dried herbs, onions, onion powder, garlic, garlic powder, dried spices, fresh or dried chiles, etc. to create the flavor profile you are looking for.

Spice rubs can be applied to the meat just before cooking or well in advance. The longer the rub sits on the meat, the more deeply its flavor will permeate. Scoring the meat lightly will help the flavors to penetrate deeply. You'll need about 2 tablespoons of spice rub for each 1 pound of meat.

MARINADES

Marinating not only adds flavor to meat, but it also tenderizes it. Generally speaking, marinades contain three types of ingredients. Acidic ingredients, such as wine, liquor, vinegar, or citrus juice do double duty, both tenderizing and flavoring the meat. Aromatics, including garlic and spices, add intense flavor elements to a dish. Oils or fats serve to keep the flavors in contact with the food so that they penetrate it. A good marinade includes all three of these ingredient types, but you can get creative and mix and match them however you please.

All meat, poultry, and fish can benefit from the flavoring effects of a good marinade. Tougher meats, such as brisket or pork shoulder get double the benefits in both added flavor and a tenderizing effect. For these meats, a long rest in the marinade is advised—anywhere from 8 hours to as long as 24 hours or even more in some cases. A whole chicken is best marinated for 4–6 hours and chicken pieces for about 2 hours. Fish or shellfish are delicate and need only a short marinating time—15–30 minutes is usually long enough for the flavors of the marinade to permeate the fish. Too long and a delicate meat will become mushy.

Always marinate in a nonreactive container, such as glass, ceramic, plastic, or stainless steel bowl. Whether you are marinating your food for 15 minutes or overnight, cover it well and keep it in the refrigerator.

GLAZES

Glazing is done at the end of cooking. Glazes tend to be thick sauces with a high sugar content, such as barbecue sauces. If you put a glaze on food early on when grilling, the sugar will burn. Instead, save your glaze until just before the food is cooked, then baste it on generously. Continue to cook briefly, just until the glaze is hot and bubbly.

BBQ Rub

MAKES ½ CUP

PREP: 5 MINS

COOK: NO COOKING

INGREDIENTS

¼ cup firmly packed dark brown sugar

1 tablespoon dry mustard

1 tablespoon salt

1 tablespoon pepper

2 teaspoons paprika

1 teaspoon dried thyme

1 teaspoon dried oregano

1 teaspoon cayenne pepper

1 teaspoon ground allspice

1. Mix all the ingredients together in a small bowl until thoroughly combined.

2. Rub the mixture thoroughly into meat, poultry, or fish just before cooking, if short of time, or up to 24 hours before cooking. If using for the maximum length of time, exclude the salt from the rub mixture and sprinkle it separately over the meat just before cooking.

3. Put into a shallow dish, cover tightly, and chill in the refrigerator until required.

Cajun Rub

MAKES ¼ CUP

PREP: 5 MINS

COOK: NO COOKING

INGREDIENTS

1 tablespoon cracked black peppercorns

2 teaspoons paprika

2 teaspoons garlic powder or crushed garlic

2 teaspoons salt

1 teaspoon dried thyme

1 teaspoon dried oregano

1 teaspoon dry mustard

½ teaspoon cayenne pepper

1. Mix all the ingredients together in a small bowl until thoroughly combined.

2. Rub the mixture thoroughly into meat, poultry, or fish just before cooking, if short of time, or for several hours before cooking.

3. Put into a shallow dish, cover tightly, and chill in the refrigerator until required.

Jamaican Jerk Rub

☆ MAKES ⅓ CUP ☆   PREP: 5 MINS   COOK: NO COOKING

INGREDIENTS

4 teaspoons packed dark brown sugar

4 teaspoons chopped fresh thyme

4 teaspoons salt

2 teaspoons ground allspice

1 teaspoon cayenne pepper or chili powder

generous pinch of freshly grated nutmeg

pinch of ground cloves

1. Mix all the ingredients together in a small bowl until thoroughly combined.

2. Rub the mixture thoroughly into meat, poultry, or fish at least 2 hours, or up to 24 hours, before cooking. If using for the maximum length of time, exclude the salt from the rub mixture and sprinkle it separately over the meat just before cooking.

3. Put into a shallow dish, cover tightly, and chill in the refrigerator until required.

Texan Rub

☆ MAKES ¼ CUP ☆   PREP: 5 MINS   COOK: NO COOKING

INGREDIENTS

1 tablespoon ground dried mild chiles

1 tablespoon onion powder

1 tablespoon dry mustard

1 tablespoon salt

1. Mix all the ingredients together in a small bowl until thoroughly combined.

2. Rub the mixture thoroughly into meat, poultry, or fish just before cooking, if short of time, or up to 24 hours before cooking. If using for the maximum length of time, exclude the salt from the rub mixture and sprinkle it separately over the meat just before cooking.

3. Put into a shallow dish, cover tightly, and chill in the refrigerator until required.

Creole Rub

☆ MAKES ⅔ CUP ☆

PREP: 5 MINS

COOK: NO COOKING

INGREDIENTS

2 tablespoons pepper

2 tablespoons celery salt

2 tablespoons paprika

4 teaspoons garlic powder

4 teaspoons dried thyme

2 teaspoons dried oregano

2 teaspoons ground bay leaves

pinch of chili powder

1. Mix all the ingredients together in a small bowl until thoroughly combined.

2. Rub the mixture thoroughly into meat, poultry, or fish 1–2 hours before cooking.

3. Put into a shallow dish, cover tightly, and chill in the refrigerator until required.

Habanero Rub

☆ MAKES ⅔ CUP ☆

PREP: 5 MINS

COOK: NO COOKING

INGREDIENTS

2 tablespoons paprika

1–2 tablespoons dried crushed habanero chiles

1 tablespoon garlic powder

1 tablespoon onion powder

1 tablespoon ground cumin

1 tablespoon salt

2 teaspoons pepper

1 teaspoon cayenne pepper

2 teaspoons packed light brown sugar

½ teaspoon freshly grated nutmeg

1. Mix all the ingredients together in a small bowl until thoroughly combined.

2. Rub the mixture thoroughly into the meat, poultry, or fish 1–2 hours before cooking.

3. Put into a shallow dish, cover tightly, and chill in the refrigerator until required.

Mediterranean Rub

★ MAKES ⅔ CUP ★   PREP: 5 MINS   COOK: NO COOKING

INGREDIENTS

grated zest of 1 orange

grated zest of 1 lemon

3 garlic cloves, crushed

¼ cup chopped fresh rosemary

2 tablespoons chopped fresh sage

1 tablespoon chopped fresh thyme

1 tablespoon salt

2 teaspoons pepper

1. Mix all the ingredients together in a small bowl until thoroughly combined.

2. Rub the mixture thoroughly into meat, poultry, or fish at least 2 hours, or up to 24 hours, before cooking. If using for the maximum length of time, exclude the salt from the rub mixture and sprinkle it separately over the meat just before cooking.

3. Put into a shallow, nonmetallic dish, cover tightly, and chill in the refrigerator until required.

Sichuan Peppercorn Rub

★ MAKES ⅓ CUP ★   PREP: 10 MINS   COOK: 5 MINS

INGREDIENTS

2 tablespoons Szechuan peppercorns

2 tablespoons coriander seeds

1 teaspoon allspice berries

1 teaspoon salt

1. Put the peppercorns and coriander seeds into a skillet and cook over medium—high heat for 2 minutes, or until fragrant. Remove from the pan and let cool, discarding any blackened peppercorns.

2. Put the peppercorns and coriander seeds with the allspice and salt into a food processor and process until crushed to a coarse powder. Don't process for too long, otherwise the mixture will become oily.

3. Rub the mixture thoroughly into meat, poultry, or fish at least 2 hours before cooking. Put into a shallow dish, cover tightly, and chill in the refrigerator until required.

Sticky BBQ Marinade

MAKES 1 CUP

PREP: 5 MINS

COOK: 5 MINS

INGREDIENTS

¼ cup firmly packed light or dark brown sugar

½ cup plum preserves

2 tablespoons tomato paste

2 tablespoons white wine vinegar

1 tablespoon whole-grain mustard

1. Heat all the ingredients in a saucepan over low heat, stirring until smooth. Remove from the heat and let cool.

2. Meanwhile, score the meat, poultry, or fish deeply with a sharp knife. Put the prepared meat, poultry, or fish into a nonmetallic dish or plastic food bag.

3. Pour the marinade over the prepared meat, poultry, or fish and turn to coat.

4. Cover tightly or seal and let marinate in the refrigerator, turning occasionally, for at least an hour or preferably, for only meat, overnight before cooking.

Spicy Beer Marinade

MAKES 2 CUPS

PREP: 5 MINS

COOK: NO COOKING

INGREDIENTS

1½ cups beer

½ cup soy sauce

1 tablespoon Worcestershire sauce

1 teaspoon hot pepper sauce

1 garlic clove, finely chopped

1 tablespoon whole-grain mustard

2 teaspoons paprika

1 teaspoon salt

1 teaspoon pepper

1. Score the meat or game pieces deeply with a sharp knife. Put the prepared meat or game into a shallow, nonmetallic dish or plastic food bag.

2. Mix all the ingredients together in a small bowl until thoroughly combined.

3. Pour the marinade over the prepared meat or game and turn to coat.

4. Cover tightly or seal and let marinate in the refrigerator, turning occasionally, for up to 6 hours before cooking.

Satay Marinade

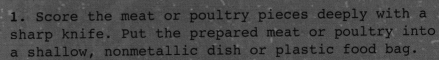

☆ MAKES 1 CUP ☆

PREP: 5 MINS

COOK: 5 MINS

INGREDIENTS

4 scallions, chopped

1 garlic clove, chopped

2 teaspoons chopped ginger

⅓ cup peanut butter

1 teaspoon packed light brown sugar

1 teaspoon Thai fish sauce

2 tablespoons soy sauce

1 tablespoon chili sauce

1 teaspoon lemon juice

salt, to taste

peanuts, to garnish

1. Score the meat or poultry pieces deeply with a sharp knife. Put the prepared meat or poultry into a shallow, nonmetallic dish or plastic food bag.

2. Put all the ingredients into a food processor. Add ⅔ cup water and process to a puree.

3. Transfer to a saucepan, season with salt, and heat gently, stirring occasionally. Let cool, then pour the marinade over the prepared meat or poultry and turn to coat.

4. Cover and let marinate in the refrigerator, turning occasionally, for up to 6 hours before cooking. Garnish with peanuts and serve.

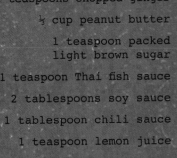

Chimichurri Marinade

☆ MAKES 1 CUP ☆

PREP: 5 MINS

COOK: NO COOKING

INGREDIENTS

½ cup white wine vinegar

3 tablespoons olive oil

2 jalapeño chiles

2 garlic cloves

1 teaspoon paprika

1 teaspoon salt

½ teaspoon ground bay leaves

1 tablespoon each chopped cilantro and parsley

2 teaspoons chopped oregano

1. Score the meat or poultry pieces deeply with a sharp knife. Put the prepared meat or poultry into a shallow, nonmetallic dish or plastic food bag.

2. Put all the ingredients, except the chopped herbs, into a food processor or blender and process until smooth and combined. Stir in the herbs.

3. Pour the marinade over the prepared meat or poultry and turn to coat.

4. Cover tightly or seal and let marinate in the refrigerator, turning occasionally, for up to 6 hours before cooking.

Chapter 2
BEEF

Beef Brisket
with Spicy Ginger Rub

★ SERVES 6–8 ★

COOK: 10 HOURS

PREP: 20 MINS
+ MARINATING
+ RESTING

INGREDIENTS

4½ pounds beef brisket

SOY & GINGER RUB

½ cup firmly packed brown sugar

⅔ cup light soy sauce

⅔ cup mirin (Japanese rice wine) or sherry

2 tablespoons Korean chili bean paste

4 garlic cloves, crushed

1 cup sliced fresh ginger

1 teaspoon pepper

1 teaspoon Sichuan peppercorns

3 star anise

1 cinnamon stick

---

1. To make the rub, mix all the ingredients together in a large bowl. Add the brisket and stir until the beef is coated thoroughly.

2. Put the brisket into a tight-fitting, nonmetallic dish and pour over any remaining rub from the bowl.

3. Cover with plastic wrap and put into the refrigerator for at least 24 hours to marinate.

4. Remove the brisket from the refrigerator at least an hour before you want to cook it, so it reaches room temperature.

5. Prepare the barbecue grill for smoking and preheat to low.

6. Place the brisket on the grill rack, point side up, and smoke for 10 hours with the lid on, or until the center of the meat is no longer pink and the juices run clear.

7. Cover the beef in aluminum foil and rest in a warm place for 30 minutes before slicing and serving.

WHEN SMOKING MEATS, IT'S ALWAYS GOOD TO PLAN A FEW DAYS AHEAD, BECAUSE IT CAN BE A LENGTHY PROCESS.

Cuts of beef

CHUCK

This portion of
the cow has more
collagen than
the other parts,
which gives it
plenty of flavor.
Because it is
also quite lean,
steaks cut from
the chuck are best
cooked using "wet"
cooking methods,
such as braising
or marinating, to
tenderize the meat
before grilling.
Chuck is also
ideal for use as
ground beef.

RIB

These premium cuts (including
prime rib and rib-eye steaks)
are tender, juicy, and full
of great marbling, making
them perfect candidates for
cooking over dry heat, such
as on a barbecue or grill.

BRISKET

This is tougher meat, best for
braising in stews, low-and-slow
barbecuing, or smoking.

SHANK

The toughest cut of all, this
meat is usually reserved for
slow braising and stews.

PLATE

Relatively tough and high in
fat, meat from this part of
the animal is best braised
(short ribs) or tenderized in
a marinade and then grilled
or seared (skirt and hanger
steaks).

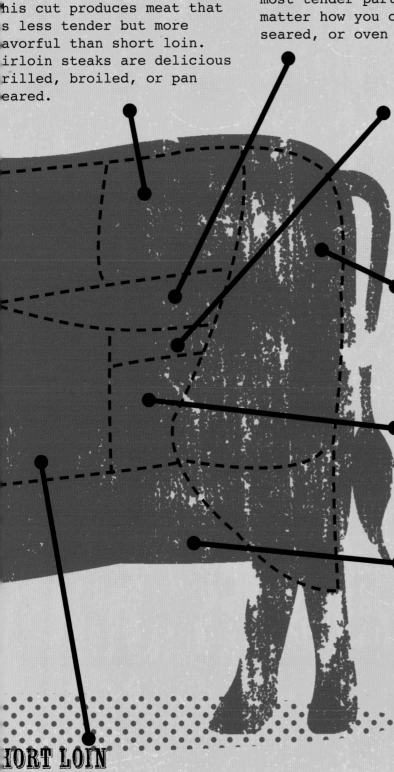

TENDERLOIN

This lean meat comes from a part of the cow that doesn't bear the animal's weight, making it the most tender part. These cuts are delicious no matter how you cook them—grilled, broiled, pan seared, or oven roasted.

IRLOIN

his cut produces meat that s less tender but more avorful than short loin. irloin steaks are delicious rilled, broiled, or pan eared.

TOP SIRLOIN

This lean cut has less marbling than the more prized cuts (such as those from the tenderloin); this is affordable and with a little pounding or marinating, makes for a tasty steak, whether grilled, broiled, or pan seared.

ROUND

This portion contains meat that is lean, somewhat tough, and with little marbling. Marinating will help to tenderize the meat, as will moist cooking methods, such as braising.

BOTTOM SIRLOIN

This portion is similar to top sirloin, but leaner and less tender. These cuts are best marinated and then grilled or oven roasted.

FLANK

With a lot of connective tissue, this cut is tougher than premium cuts, but very flavorful. Much of the flank is used for grinding into ground beef. The flank steak is great for grilling, provided it is first well tenderized in a marinade.

ORT LOIN

ese well-marbled cuts produce tender, juicy, and vorful steaks on the grill. All but the T-bone are so ideal for searing in a pan (the bone in a T-bone kes consistent pan searing difficult).

Beef Rib-Eye Steaks
with Caper & Anchovy Butter

★ SERVES 4 ★

PREP: 30 MINS
+ RESTING

COOK:
20 MINS

INGREDIENTS

¼ cup olive oil

1 teaspoon salt

1 teaspoon pepper

2 beef rib-eye steaks,
each weighing 1¾ pounds

CAPER & ANCHOVY BUTTER

5 anchovy fillets,
chopped

1¾ sticks butter,
softened

2 garlic cloves, crushed

⅓ cup baby capers

small bunch of fresh
parsley, chopped

1 teaspoon salt

1 teaspoon pepper

1. Put the oil, salt, and pepper into a nonmetallic dish large enough to fit the steaks in. Add the steaks and turn a few times to coat thoroughly. Set aside.

2. To make the butter, put all the ingredients into a medium bowl. Beat well with a wooden spoon until well combined.

3. Prepare the barbecue grill for direct cooking and preheat to medium-hot.

4. Place the steaks on the grill rack and cook for 10 minutes on each side for medium-rare, or to your preference. Turn every now and then and brush with the butter until the steaks are well coated.

5. When the steaks are cooked, cover with aluminum foil and let rest in a warm place for 5 minutes. Slice and serve with any remaining butter on the side.

1

2

5

THE CAPER & ANCHOVY BUTTER
ALSO GOES WELL
WITH ANY MEATY FISH, SUCH
AS TUNA, SALMON, SWORDFISH,
OR MACKEREL.

T-Bone Steak
with Mushroom Butter

 ★ SERVES 4 ★

 PREP: 25 MINS
+ CHILLING
+ RESTING

 COOK: 25 MINS

INGREDIENTS

2 large red onions, sliced into 1-inch-thick circles

olive oil, for brushing

4 T-bone steaks, 1-inch thick

salt and pepper, to taste

MUSHROOM BUTTER

1 stick unsalted butter, softened

1 shallot, diced

1 ounce mushrooms, such as porcini, chanterelle, cremini, or a mixture, diced

1 tablespoon chopped fresh thyme leaves or 1 teaspoon dried thyme

1 teaspoon salt

½ teaspoon pepper

1 tablespoon red wine

1. To make the mushroom butter, melt 2 tablespoons of the butter in a large, heavy skillet over medium-high heat. Add the shallot and cook for about 5 minutes, stirring occasionally, until translucent. Add the mushrooms, thyme, salt, and pepper and continue to cook for another 5 minutes, stirring occasionally, until the mushrooms are soft and beginning to brown. Add the wine and stir for 30 seconds to deglaze the pan. Set aside to cool for a few minutes.

2. In a food processor, combine the remaining butter with the mushroom mixture. Scoop out onto a square of wax paper, form into a log, wrap, and chill for about 30 minutes, or until firm.

3. Prepare the barbecue grill for direct cooking and preheat to hot. Brush the onions with oil and season the steaks and the onions all over with salt and pepper. Place the steaks and onions on the grill rack and cook for about 5 minutes on each side for medium-rare, or until the onions are soft and slightly charred.

4. Remove from the grill, top each steak with a few pats of mushroom butter, and let rest for about 5 minutes. Serve topped with more mushroom butter and a few charred onion rings.

THIS DELICIOUS MELTED
MUSHROOM BUTTER MAKES A
GREAT SAUCE FOR ANY STEAK
AT A BARBECUE.

Chuck Steak
with Black Bean Salsa

 SERVES 4

PREP: 25 MINS

 COOK: 8 MINS

INGREDIENTS

¼ cup olive oil

1 teaspoon salt

1 teaspoon pepper

4 chuck steaks, each
weighing 12 ounces

BLACK BEAN SALSA

1 (15-ounce) can black
beans, drained

2 cups drained
canned corn kernels

1 small red onion,
finely chopped

1 green bell pepper,
seeded and chopped

1 tablespoon
chipotle paste

1 tablespoon packed
light brown sugar

small bunch of fresh
cilantro, chopped

¼ cup extra virgin
olive oil

2 tablespoons
sherry vinegar

1 teaspoon salt

1 teaspoon pepper

1. To make the salsa, mix together all of the ingredients in a medium bowl. Let rest for 10 minutes for the flavors to mingle, then put into the refrigerator.

2. Prepare the barbecue grill for direct cooking and preheat to hot.

3. Put the oil, salt, and pepper into a nonmetallic dish large enough to fit the steaks in. Add the steaks and turn a few times to coat thoroughly.

4. Place the steaks on the grill rack and cook for 4 minutes on each side for medium-rare, or to your preference.

5. Rest the steaks in a warm place for a couple of minutes before slicing and serving with the salsa.

IF YOU LIKE YOUR STEAK
COOKED A LITTLE MORE, TRY
USING RIB-EYE INSTEAD
OF CHUCK.

Smoked Beef
Short Ribs

 SERVES 4

 PREP: 20 MINS
+ BRINING
+ RESTING

 COOK:
6 HOURS

INGREDIENTS

2 racks beef short ribs,
about 2¼ pounds each,
membrane removed (ask
your butcher to do this)

¼ cup packed light
brown sugar

2 tablespoons old bay
seasoning

SALT MARINADE

10½ cups water

2 cups sea salt crystals

1¼ cups firmly packed
brown sugar

10 cloves

20 peppercorns

small bunch of
fresh thyme

3 cinnamon sticks

3 star anise

10½ cups iced water

1. To make the salt marinade, put the water, salt, sugar, cloves, peppercorns, thyme, cinnamon sticks, and star anise into a large saucepan. Bring to a boil until the salt has dissolved. Turn off the heat and then add the iced water.

2. Put the ribs into a large, nonmetallic container and pour the marinade over them. Put a plate on top to keep the ribs submerged. Cover and place in the refrigerator for 24 hours. Remove the ribs from the marinade at least an hour before you want to cook them, so they reach room temperature.

3. Put the ribs onto a board and rub in the sugar and old bay seasoning.

4. Prepare the barbecue grill for smoking and preheat to low. Cook, meat side up, covered with a lid, for 6 hours, or until the center of the meat is no longer pink and the juices run clear. Cover with aluminum foil and let rest for 30 minutes before serving.

 2

 3

 4

MARINATING IN A SALT SOLUTION TAKES A WHILE, SO IT'S A GOOD IDEA TO MARINATE EXTRA AND FREEZE THEM. THEY WILL KEEP FOR SEVERAL MONTHS.

Rib-Eye Steak
with Ranch Dressing

SERVES 4

PREP: 20 MINS

COOK: 3 MINS

INGREDIENTS

¼ cup olive oil

1 teaspoon salt

1 teaspoon pepper

4 rib-eye steaks, each about 10 ounces

RANCH DRESSING

1 tablespoon mayonnaise

1 tablespoon sour cream

1 tablespoon buttermilk

1 tablespoon apple cider vinegar

1 teaspoon Dijon mustard

1 garlic clove, crushed

4 fresh chives, snipped

sprig of fresh parsley, chopped

sprig of fresh dill, chopped

½ teaspoon salt

½ teaspoon pepper

1. Prepare the barbecue grill for direct cooking and preheat to hot.

2. Put the olive oil, salt, and pepper into a nonmetallic dish large enough to fit all of the steaks. Add the steaks, turning them a few times to coat thoroughly.

3. To make the dressing, whisk together all of the ingredients in a small bowl. Set aside.

4. Place the steaks on the grill rack and cook for 4 minutes on each side for medium-rare, or until cooked to your preference.

5. Rest the steaks for 2 minutes, then serve with the dressing.

ALWAYS MAKE SURE YOUR STEAKS ARE AT ROOM TEMPERATURE BEFORE YOU COOK THEM, BECAUSE THIS HELPS THEM TO COOK MORE EVENLY.

Sirloin Steak Fajitas

SERVES 4

PREP: 20 MINS
+ MARINATING

COOK:
10-15 MINS

INGREDIENTS

1 sirloin steak,
about 1½ pounds and
¾ inch thick

4 wheat tortillas

2 tomatoes,
thinly sliced

1 avocado, peeled,
pitted, and sliced

¼ cup sour cream

4 scallions,
thinly sliced

MARINADE

2 tablespoons sunflower
oil, plus extra for
oiling

finely grated zest of
1 lime

1 tablespoon lime juice

2 garlic cloves, crushed

¼ teaspoon ground
coriander

¼ teaspoon ground cumin

pinch of sugar

1. To make the marinade, put all the marinade ingredients into a dish, mix together, and add the steak. Turn to coat thoroughly and marinate for 6—8 hours, turning occasionally.

2. Prepare the barbecue grill for indirect cooking and preheat to hot. Oil the grill rack.

3. Remove the steak from the marinade and cook on the hottest part of the rack for 2—3 minutes on each side. Move to the cooler part and cook the steak to your preference. Transfer to a board and let rest for 5 minutes.

4. Meanwhile, warm the tortillas. Thinly slice the steak and arrange on the tortillas. Add the tomato, avocado, sour cream, and scallions. Fold over and serve immediately.

Porterhouse Steak
in Red Wine Sauce

PREP: 25 MINS

COOK: 30 MINS

INGREDIENTS

2 tablespoons olive oil

1 teaspoon salt

1 teaspoon pepper

2 porterhouse steaks,
each about 12 ounces

RED WINE SAUCE

1 tablespoon olive oil

1 tablespoon butter

1 red onion,
finely chopped

2 garlic cloves, crushed

small bunch of fresh
thyme, chopped

1 cup red wine

1 tablespoon flour

1 teaspoon Dijon mustard

1 teaspoon tomato paste

1 cup beef stock
or broth

salt and pepper,
to taste

1. Put the olive oil, salt, and pepper into a nonmetallic dish large enough to fit both of the steaks. Add the steaks, turning them a few times to coat thoroughly.

2. To make the red wine sauce, heat the olive oil and butter in a medium saucepan over medium heat. Add the red onion and garlic and cook for 10 minutes, stirring every now and then until translucent and caramelized. Add the thyme and red wine and simmer until reduced by half, then add the flour, mustard, and tomato paste. Slowly add the stock, stirring continually to avoid any lumps, then season with salt and pepper. When the sauce has cooked for a couple of minutes, turn off the heat and keep in a warm place.

3. Prepare the barbecue grill for direct cooking and preheat to hot.

4. Place the steaks on the grill rack and cook for 4 minutes on each side for medium-rare, or cook to your preference. Let the steaks rest for 2 minutes in a warm place then serve with the red wine sauce.

ALWAYS TRY TO BUY AGED BEEF, BECAUSE IT HAS A MUCH BETTER FLAVOR AND IS MORE TENDER.

Cheddar-Jalapeño
Hamburgers

 SERVES 4

 PREP: 20 MINS

 COOK: 10-15 MINS

INGREDIENTS

675 g/1 lb 8 oz lean fresh beef mince

1 extra-large egg, lightly beaten

2 scallions, thinly sliced

1–2 jalapeño chiles, seeded and finely chopped

2 tablespoons finely chopped fresh cilantro

2 tablespoons Worcestershire sauce

½ teaspoon salt

½ teaspoon pepper

115 g/4 oz mature Cheddar cheese, grated

TO SERVE

4 burger buns, halved and toasted

tomato slices

lettuce

ketchup

1. In a large bowl, combine the beef, egg, scallions, chiles, cilantro, Worcestershire sauce, salt, and pepper. Form the mixture into eight equal-sized balls and flatten them into burgers about 1 cm/½ inch thick. Top half of the burgers with grated cheese, leaving a clear border around the edge of each burger.

2. Prepare the barbecue for direct cooking and preheat to medium—hot.

3. Place the remaining four burgers on top of the cheese-topped burgers and press the edges together to enclose the cheese. Flatten again into burgers 1–2 cm/½–¾ inch thick, making sure that the edges are well sealed.

4. Place the burgers on the barbecue grill and cook for about 5—8 minutes on each side, or until the center of the meat is no longer pink and the juices run clear. Serve on the toasted burger buns with tomato slices, lettuce, and ketchup.

THE MOLTEN CHEESE CENTER
KEEPS THESE FLAVORSOME
BURGERS NICE AND JUICY.

Brisket Philly Cheesesteak

 SERVES 4

 PREP: 20 MINS

 COOK: 5½ HOURS

INGREDIENTS

1 kg/2 lb 4 oz beef brisket

2 teaspoons salt

2 teaspoons pepper

4 sub rolls

¼ cup mayonnaise

FILLING

2 tablespoons oil

2 tablespoons butter

2 green bell peppers, sliced

1 onion, sliced

1 teaspoon salt

1 teaspoon pepper

600 g/1 lb 5 oz pizza mozzarella, grated

1. Prepare the barbecue for indirect cooking and preheat to medium-low.

2. Put the beef on a board and gently rub in the salt and pepper.

3. Place the beef point-side up on the barbecue grill and cook for 5 hours with the lid on. Check that the beef is cooked through and the juices run clear. Remove from the barbecue and let cool completely.

4. To make the filling, heat the oil and butter in a skillet and cook the peppers and onion over medium heat for 10 minutes, or until the vegetables are soft to the touch. Sprinkle with the salt and pepper.

5. Preheat a grill to high. Slice the beef as thinly as possible and divide into four piles on a baking tray. Top each beef pile with the peppers, onions and grated cheese. Grill until all of the cheese has melted.

6. Cut the sub rolls in half lengthwise, spread with the mayonnaise and then fill with piles of the beef mixture. Serve immediately.

CAN'T FIND SUB ROLLS? TRY USING SMALL FRENCH STICKS OR A LARGE FRENCH STICK CUT INTO FOUR.

Beef Sausages
with Scorched Tomato Relish

 SERVES 4 ✫

 PREP: 30 MINS + CHILLING

 COOK: 35-40 MINS

INGREDIENTS

SAUSAGES

2 pounds beef chuck, diced and chilled

½ cup beef suet

2 teaspoons fennel seeds

2 teaspoons dried thyme

small bunch of fresh parsley, chopped

1 tablespoon Dijon mustard

2 teaspoons salt

1 teaspoon pepper

1 tablespoon tomato paste

3½-foot sausage casing

SCORCHED TOMATO RELISH

¼ cup olive oil

2 tablespoons red wine vinegar

1 tablespoon sugar

4 large tomatoes, halved

1 red bell pepper, halved and seeded

1 red onion, quartered

1 large red chile

4 garlic cloves

handful of fresh parsley

1 teaspoon salt

1 teaspoon pepper

1. To make the sausages, mix the diced beef with the suet, fennel seeds, thyme, parsley, mustard, salt, pepper, and tomato paste in a large bowl.

2. Using a meat grinder, grind the beef mixture, using the course grinding plate. Refrigerate the ground meat for 30 minutes.

3. Soak the sausage casing according to the package directions. Thread the casing onto a sausage stuffer and tie off the end. Fill the sausage stuffer with the chilled filling.

4. Hold the casing steady and fill with the filling. When the casing is filled, lay the sausage down in a straight line and prick all the way along with a pin. Turn over and repeat on the other side. Twist and snip into four long sausages.

5. Prepare the barbecue grill for direct cooking and preheat to medium-hot.

6. To make the relish, mix all the ingredients in a large bowl, then transfer to a baking pan. Place on the grill rack and cook with the lid on for 25 minutes, or until all the vegetables are slightly charred and softened. Let cool slightly.

7. Put all the cooled vegetables onto a cutting board and chop with a knife into a coarse relish. Put the sausages on the grill rack for 6 minutes on each side, or until the center of the sausage is no longer pink and the juices run clear. Serve the sausages immediately with the relish.

TRY USING HEIRLOOM TOMATOES
AND POBLANO CHILES FOR A
MORE UNUSUAL RELISH.

Chapter 3
PORK & LAMB

Pulled Pork
with Mashed Sweet Potatoes

 ☆ SERVES 6-8 ☆

 PREP: 20 MINS + RESTING

 COOK: 12¼ HOURS

INGREDIENTS

6½ pounds pork shoulder, skin removed and bone in

RUB

1 tablespoon paprika

2 tablespoons packed light brown sugar

1 teaspoon dried thyme

1 teaspoon dried oregano

2 teaspoons pepper

1 teaspoon garlic salt

1 teaspoon celery salt

1 teaspoon salt

1 teaspoon onion powder

CHILI SAUCE

2 tablespoons yellow mustard

2 tablespoons apple cider vinegar

2 tablespoons molasses

2 tablespoons ketchup

1 tablespoon sriracha chili sauce

MASHED SWEET POTATOES

4 sweet potatoes, diced

1¾ sticks salted butter, diced

1 teaspoon pepper

1. Prepare the barbecue grill for smoking and preheat to low.

2. Combine together all of the rub ingredients in a small bowl.

3. Put the pork onto a cutting board and massage the rub all over the meat.

4. Place the pork on the grill rack, making sure the pork is fat side up. Close the lid and cook for 12 hours, or until a thick dark golden crust has formed. Check that the center of the meat is no longer pink and the juices run clear. Cover in aluminum foil and let rest in a warm place for 30 minutes.

5. Mix together the mustard, vinegar, molasses, ketchup, and chili sauce in a small bowl. Set aside.

6. Boil or steam the sweet potatoes in a large saucepan until soft when pricked with a knife. Drain and mash, then beat in the butter and pepper.

7. Remove any bones from the pork and pull the meat into large chunks; the meat should be tender, so it should not be hard to do. Put the pork into a large bowl and pour the chili sauce over it. Gently mix, trying not to break the pork up too much.

8. Serve the pork with the mashed sweet potatoes.

TRY TO START COOKING YOUR
PORK BEGINNING EARLY IN
THE MORNING TO AVOID HAVING
TO EAT LATE.

Baby Back Ribs
with Old Bay Rub

SERVES 4

PREP: 20 MINS
+ MARINATING

COOK:
4 HOURS

INGREDIENTS

4 racks baby back pork
ribs, each weighing
1 pound

SPICY MARINADE

2 tablespoons packed
light brown sugar

3 tablespoons old bay
seasoning

1 tablespoon
Worcestershire sauce

4 teaspoons salt

APPLE GLAZE

⅔ cup apple juice

2 tablespoons olive oil

2 tablespoons apple
cider vinegar

1. To make the spicy marinade, mix together all the ingredients in a large bowl, then add the pork ribs and turn to coat thoroughly.

2. Put the ribs into a nonmetallic dish, adding any remaining marinade from the bowl. Cover the dish with plastic wrap and put into the refrigerator for at least 12 hours to marinate.

3. Remove the ribs from the refrigerator at least an hour before you want to cook them, so they can reach room temperature.

4. To make the apple glaze, mix together the apple juice, olive oil, and apple cider vinegar in a small bowl and set aside.

5. Prepare the barbecue grill for indirect cooking and preheat to medium-low.

6. Cook the ribs on the grill rack for 4 hours, with the lid on. Brush the ribs on each side with the apple glaze every 30 minutes.

7. When the ribs are cooked through and the meat is falling off the bone, remove from the grill. Check that the center of the meat is no longer pink and the juices run clear, then serve immediately.

PORK RIBS TEND TO GET STUCK
IN YOUR TEETH, SO IT'S ALWAYS
GOOD TO HAVE SOME TOOTHPICKS
ON HAND.

Apple-Glazed Pork Chops

 SERVES 4

 PREP: 20 MINS

 COOK: 20 MINS

INGREDIENTS

¼ cup olive oil

1 teaspoon salt

1 teaspoon pepper

4 pork chops, each
weighing about 12 ounces

APPLE GLAZE

3 large Granny Smith or
other cooking apples,
peeled, cored, and
chopped

2 tablespoons sugar

juice of 1 lemon

⅔ cup hard dry cider
or apple juice

1. In a nonmetallic dish wide enough to hold all the pork chops, stir together the oil, salt, and pepper. Add the pork chops and turn a few times to coat thoroughly. Set aside.

2. To make the apple glaze, put the apples, sugar, lemon juice, and cider into a medium saucepan with a lid on. Cook over medium heat for 5 minutes, stirring occasionally.

3. When the apples are softened and starting to fall apart, remove from the heat and let cool slightly.

4. Prepare the barbecue grill for direct cooking and preheat to medium-hot.

5. Using a handheld blender, blend the apple mixture into a smooth glaze.

6. Cook the chops on the grill rack for 6 minutes on each side, brushing with the apple glaze as they cook.

7. When the chops are cooked through, or when the center of the meat is no longer pink and the juices run clear, brush with the glaze one last time and serve immediately.

THIS DISH MAKES A GREAT
ADDITION TO A SUMMER
BARBECUE IN SEPTEMBER,
ESPECIALLY IF YOU HAVE A
BUMPER CROP OF APPLES TO USE.

BBQ Pork Spareribs

SERVES 4

PREP: 30 MINS
+ MARINATING
+ RESTING

COOK:
2–2½ HOURS

INGREDIENTS

1 (4–5 pound) rack
pork spareribs

1 onion, quartered

2 bay leaves

2 teaspoon whole blacks
peppercorns

1 teaspoon salt

Classic BBQ Sauce
(see page 166)

1. Place the ribs in a large saucepan (cut the rack in half, if necessary) and cover with cold water. Add the onion, bay leaves, peppercorns, and salt and bring to a boil over high heat. Reduce the heat to low and simmer for 1½–2 hours, testing occasionally during the last 30 minutes of cooking. Remove from the heat once the meat begins to pull apart with little resistance. Drain the ribs, discarding the onion, peppercorns, and bay leaves.

2. Coat the ribs with some of the barbecue sauce, then cover and refrigerate for 2–8 hours. Remove from the refrigerator 30 minutes before you are ready to start cooking.

3. Prepare the barbecue grill for direct cooking and preheat to hot. Baste the ribs with more barbecue sauce. Place on the grill rack and cook for 12–15 minutes on each side, turning and basting every 5–10 minutes, until the sauce is caramelized and just beginning to blacken in places. Check that the center of the meat is no longer pink and the juices run clear.

4. Remove from the grill rack and let stand for 5 minutes. Cut into individual ribs and serve immediately.

1

2

3

THESE MEATY PORK SPARERIBS
ARE PERFECT FOR A PARTY AND
ARE FINGER-LICKIN' GOOD!

Maple-Mustard Pork
with Grilled Peaches

★ SERVES 4 ★

PREP: 20 MINS + MARINATING

COOK: 1¼ HOURS

INGREDIENTS

2¾–3 pounds boneless pork loin

4 small, ripe but firm peaches, pitted and halved

MARINADE

½ cup maple syrup

½ cup Dijon mustard

2 garlic cloves, finely chopped

2 tablespoons apple cider vinegar

1 tablespoon finely chopped fresh thyme

¾ teaspoon salt

½ teaspoon pepper

1. To make the marinade, combine all the ingredients in a large bowl. Add the pork, toss to coat, cover, and marinate in the refrigerator for at least 2 hours or up to 24 hours.

2. Prepare the barbecue grill for indirect cooking and preheat to medium-hot. Remove the pork from the marinade, reserving the marinade, and place on the hottest part of the grill rack. Cook for about 10 minutes on each side, until browned. Move the pork away from the direct heat. Cover and cook, turning every 10 minutes or so, basting with some of the reserved marinade, for an additional 45–50 minutes, until the center of the meat is no longer pink and the juices run clear. Remove the pork from the heat, cover loosely with aluminum foil, and let rest for 10 minutes.

3. Put the remaining marinade into a saucepan over high heat and bring to a boil. Reduce the heat to medium and simmer for about 8 minutes, or until the marinade thickens to form a sauce.

4. Place the peaches on the grill rack over the hottest part of the grill and cook for 2 minutes on each side, or until grill marks appear.

5. Slice the pork into ½-inch-thick slices and serve immediately, drizzled with the reduced sauce and with the grilled peach halves on the side.

MARINATING THE PORK
IN MAPLE SYRUP AND MUSTARD
OVERNIGHT GIVES THE MEAT
A FANTASTIC FLAVOR.

Braised Pork Belly
with Apple & Mustard Ketchup

 SERVES 4 ☆

 PREP: 25 MINS + RESTING

 COOK: 2¼ HOURS

INGREDIENTS

small bunch of fresh thyme

1 bulb of fennel, sliced

1 onion, sliced

3¼ pounds pork belly

2 cups hard dry cider or apple juice

1¼ cups chicken stock or broth

⅔ cup apple cider vinegar

¼ cup honey

1 teaspoon salt

1 teaspoon pepper

APPLE & MUSTARD KETCHUP

juice of 2 lemons

¼ cup sugar

3 Granny Smith or other cooking apples, peeled, cored, and chopped

2 tablespoons yellow mustard

1. Prepare the barbecue grill for indirect cooking and preheat to medium.

2. Put the thyme, fennel, and onion into a deep baking pan slightly bigger than the pork. Put the pork belly on top.

3. In a medium bowl, mix together the cider, stock, vinegar, and honey.

4. Pour the cider mixture over the pork and then sprinkle with salt and pepper.

5. Place the baking pan on the grill rack and cover the grill with the lid. Cook for 2 hours, or until the pork meat is soft to the touch and a crackling has formed. Check that the center of the meat is no longer pink and the juices run clear.

6. Put all the ketchup ingredients into a medium microwave-proof bowl. Cover with microwavable plastic wrap and cook on high for 4 minutes, or until the apples start to fall apart. Blend the ketchup with a handheld blender until smooth and let cool down.

7. When the pork is cooked, remove it from the grill and let rest in a warm place for 30 minutes. Strain the juices from the baking pan into a medium saucepan and simmer until the liquid is reduced by half.

8. Serve the pork with the cooking juices poured over the top and the ketchup on the side.

FOR THE ULTIMATE
SANDWICH, JUST CUT THE PORK
INTO SLICES AND ADD
BREAD AND COLESLAW!

Jerk Pork Tenderloin

 SERVES 4-6

 PREP: 20 MINS
+ MARINATING
+ RESTING

 COOK: 30-35 MINS

INGREDIENTS

2 pork tenderloins
of equal length, about
2¼ pounds in total

vegetable oil,
for brushing

salt and pepper,
to taste

plain boiled rice,
to serve

JERK MARINADE

3 tablespoons allspice
berries

3 cloves

¾-inch piece cinnamon
stick, broken

½ teaspoon freshly
grated nutmeg

2 large garlic cloves

1-2 fresh red chiles,
seeded and finely chopped

1 cup snipped
fresh chives

2 teaspoons sea salt

2 tablespoons malt or
apple cider vinegar

2 tablespoons soy sauce

1 tablespoon rum

1. To make the marinade, dry-roast the allspice berries in a small skillet until you smell the aroma. Using a mortar and pestle, grind to a powder with the cloves, cinnamon stick, and nutmeg. Put into a food processor with the remaining marinade ingredients. Process to a thin paste for 2 minutes.

2. Spread the marinade all over the pork, rubbing it in well. Cover with plastic wrap and let marinate in the refrigerator for 2 hours.

3. Put the pork onto a board. Brush the two upward-facing surfaces with oil. Place one of the tenderloins on top of the other, oiled sides together, to make a sandwich. Tie neatly with string at 1¾-inch intervals and brush all over with oil. Season with salt and pepper. Cover and let stand at room temperature for 30 minutes.

4. Prepare the barbecue grill for indirect cooking and preheat to hot. Oil the grill rack.

5. Place the meat on the hottest part of the grill rack and cook for 8 minutes, turning every 2 minutes, until brown on the outside. Move to the cooler part and cover with a lid. Cook for 20-25 minutes, or until the center of the meat is no longer pink and the juices run clear.

6. Transfer the meat to a board. Cover with aluminum foil and let rest for 10 minutes. Carve into slices and serve with the juices that have flowed from the meat and boiled rice.

CARVE THE COOKED PORK INTO
DIAGONAL SLICES THAT ARE
ABOUT ½ INCH THICK.

Cuts of pork

SHOULDER

Also known as pork butt or Boston butt, cuts from this area are often sold as 5—10 pound boneless roasts, suitable for braising, slow roasting, and cooking over a barbecue. This is a good cut for pulled pork recipes.

LOIN

The best part of the loin is the end nearest the head, known as the rib end. The loin supplies lean tenderloin, steaks, roasts, and chops. Country-style ribs and baby back ribs are from the loin.

LEG (HAM)

This is a lean cut that is usually cured to make ham, but fresh ham can be slow roasted carefully so it doesn't dry out.

HEAD (CHEEK)

This sweet cut should be cooked slowly to be sure it's really tender.

FOOT

The feet can be stewed, braised, or slow roasted, or they can be used for stocks.

HOCK

This cut needs to be slow cooked until the meat falls off the bone, but then it's sweet and tender.

PORK BELLY OR SIDE

Pork belly is great for roasting and is also cured as bacon. The barbecue's favorite spareribs come from this area.

PICNIC SHOULDER

Sometimes called pork arm shoulder, this tough, fatty cut is often sold bone-in; slow cooking, such as braising or smoking, is best and it is ideal for pulled pork.

Cuts of lamb

NECK

This meat is good for slow moist cooking methods such as braising or stews. There is less meat from this area, but the flavor is outstanding.

RIB

Racks of lamb from the rib section usually have seven ribs, but an eighth rib from the shoulder might be included. Divided, you have rib chops ideal for grilling.

LOIN

The area between the ribs and leg, including the sirloin, the loin is often cut into chops—loin chops are bigger than rib chops and more tender than sirloin chops—or it is boned and cut into medallions.

SHOULDER

This cut is normally sold boned, rolled, and tied, perfect for roasting, but can be found bone-in. Lamb shoulder is a good cut for braising. Shoulder chops and blade chopes can be grilled.

FORESHANK

Lean shanks from the front leg are meatier and easier to find than those from the rear legs. This cut benefits from braising.

LEG

This cut is great for roasting, grilling, or broiling, and it produces plenty of lean and tender meat. It may be sold with the rear shank for roasting bone-in, or it can be boned and butterflied; smaller cuts include chops and steaks.

BREAST

Spareribs, or lamb riblets, are the most common cut from the breast sold in grocery stores and are suitable for broiling, braising, and grilling on the barbecue. Denver ribs can be braised; breast lamb is also used for ground lamb.

Pork Belly Sliders
with Kimchi Slaw

 MAKES 14

 PREP: 20 MINS + COOLING

 COOK: 2¼ HOURS

INGREDIENTS

2¼ pounds pork belly

3 star anise

1 cinnamon stick

5 dried shiitake mushrooms

5 scallions

1 cup sugar

½ cup light soy sauce

1¼ cups mirin (Japanese) rice wine or sherry

½ cup rice vinegar

14 slider rolls (see page 182)

½ cup Japanese mayonnaise, for spreading

KIMCHI SLAW

3 tablespoons Japanese mayonnaise

¼ napa cabbage, shredded

8 ounces kimchi, sliced

4 scallions, sliced

4 teaspoons chopped pickled ginger

1. Preheat the oven to 350°F.

2. Put the pork belly, star anise, cinnamon stick, mushrooms, scallions, sugar, soy sauce, mirin, and rice vinegar into a baking dish. Cover with wax paper and aluminum foil.

3. Roast in the preheated oven for 2 hours, or until the center of the meat is no longer pink and the juices run clear. Let cool completely in the cooking liquid.

4. To make the slaw, mix together all the ingredients in a medium bowl.

5. Prepare the barbecue grill for direct cooking and preheat to medium-hot.

6. Slice the pork into ⅜-inch-thick slices. Place the slices on the grill rack and cook for 3—4 minutes on each side, or until starting to caramelize.

7. Cut the pork slices into squares. Slice the rolls in half, spread with mayonnaise, then fill with the pork and slaw.

ANY LEFTOVER PORK BELLY
FROM THIS RECIPE CAN ALSO
BE USED IN STIR-FRIES OR
NOODLE SOUPS.

Chili Hot Dogs
with Texan Chili

 SERVES 4

 PREP: 20 MINS

 COOK: 2½ HOURS

INGREDIENTS

TEXAN CHILI

¼ cup olive oil

1 onion, diced

1 celery stick, diced

2 garlic cloves, crushed

12 ounces ground beef

1 tablespoon flour

1 tablespoon paprika

1 tablespoon ground cumin

1 tablespoon ground coriander

1 teaspoon dried oregano

1 teaspoon onion powder

1 teaspoon chili powder

1 teaspoon dried thyme

1¾ cups tomato puree or sauce

1¾ cups beef stock or broth

salt and pepper, to taste

HOT DOGS

4 large frankfurters

4 hot dog buns

yellow mustard, to serve

1 onion, chopped

1. To make the chili, heat the oil in a medium saucepan and sauté the onion, celery, and garlic over low heat. Cook, with the lid on, for 10 minutes, or until the vegetables are translucent and softened.

2. Turn up the heat a little and add the beef. Cook for another 10 minutes, breaking up the meat with a wooden spoon.

3. Add the flour, paprika, cumin, coriander, oregano, onion powder, chili powder, and thyme, stirring a few times. Slowly add the tomato puree and beef stock. Season with salt and pepper and cook over low heat, with a lid, on for 2 hours, or until the meat is tender and the sauce has thickened. Turn off the heat and let rest in a warm place.

4. Prepare the barbecue grill for direct cooking and preheat to medium-hot.

5. Place the frankfurters on the grill rack and cook for 10 minutes, turning every now and then. Check that they are cooked through and the center of the meat is no longer pink.

6. Serve the frankfurters in the buns, topped with the chili, mustard, and chopped onion.

THIS CHILI CAN BE MADE
THE DAY BEFORE; IT'S ALSO
GREAT WITH BURGER BUNS
FOR A SLOPPY JOE.

Hot Link Sausages
with Pineapple Salsa

SERVES 4   PREP: 40 MINS + CHILLING   COOK: 12 MINS

INGREDIENTS

HOT LINK SAUSAGES

2¼ pounds pork shoulder, diced and chilled

2 teaspoons fennel seeds

2 tablespoons paprika

2 teaspoons dried thyme

2 teaspoons dried oregano

4 garlic cloves, chopped

2 teaspoons salt

1 teaspoon pepper

1 teaspoon crushed red pepper flakes

3½-foot sausage casing

oil, for brushing

PINEAPPLE SALSA

1 ripe pineapple

1 red onion, finely diced

1 teaspoon crushed red pepper flakes

2 tablespoons olive oil

1 tablespoon packed light brown sugar

juice of 1 lime

1 teaspoon salt

1 teaspoon pepper

small bunch of fresh cilantro, chopped

1. To make the sausages, mix the pork shoulder with all the other ingredients in a large bowl until the pork is coated thoroughly.

2. Using a meat grinder, grind the pork and other sausage ingredients using a course grinding plate. Refrigerate the ground meat for 30 minutes.

3. Soak the sausage casing according to the package directions. Thread the casing onto a sausage stuffer and tie off the end. Fill the sausage stuffer with the chilled filling.

4. Hold the casing steady and fill with the filling. When the casing is filled, lay the sausage down in a straight line and prick all the way along with a pin. Turn over and repeat on the other side. Twist and snip into four long sausages.

5. To make the salsa, cut the top and bottom off the pineapple and stand upright. Cut the skin away, making sure there aren't brown eyes left on the pineapple. Cut into four equal pieces; remove the core, then cut into ½-inch cubes. Put the pineapple and the rest of the salsa ingredients into a medium bowl and mix well. Let stand for a short while.

6. Prepare the barbecue grill for direct cooking and preheat to medium-hot. Brush the grill rack with a little oil and then cook the sausages for 6 minutes on each side, or until the center of the meat is no longer pink and the juices run clear. Serve immediately with the salsa.

IF YOU DON'T HAVE THE TIME
OR EQUIPMENT TO MAKE THE
SAUSAGES, THESE SAUSAGES CAN
BE BOUGHT ALREADY MADE.

Italian Sausage, Pepper & Onion Hoagies

 SERVES 4

 PREP: 40 MINS + CHILLING

 COOK: 20-25 MINS

INGREDIENTS

ITALIAN SAUSAGES

2¼ pounds pork shoulder, diced and chilled

2 teaspoons fennel seeds

2 teaspoons dried sage

2 teaspoons dried thyme

bunch of chopped parsley

zest of 2 lemons

2 teaspoons salt

1 teaspoon pepper

1 teaspoon crushed red pepper flakes

3½-foot sausage casing

oil, for brushing

FILLING

¼ cup olive oil

1 each red and green bell pepper, seeded and diced

1 red onion, diced

2 tablespoons red wine vinegar

1 teaspoon salt

1 teaspoon pepper

4 sub rolls

⅓ cup mayonnaise

handful of arugula

1. To make the sausages, mix the pork shoulder with all the other ingredients in a large bowl until the pork is coated thoroughly.

2. Using a meat grinder, grind the pork and other sausage ingredients using a course grinding plate. Refrigerate the ground meat for 30 minutes.

3. Soak the sausage casing according to the package directions. Thread the casing onto a sausage stuffer and tie off the end. Fill the sausage stuffer with the chilled filling.

4. Hold the casing steady and fill with the filling. When the casing is filled, lay the sausage down in a straight line and prick all the way along with a pin. Turn over and repeat on the other side. Twist and snip into four long sausages.

5. To make the filling, heat the oil in a medium skillet. Add the bell peppers and onion and cook over medium heat for 10 minutes, or until the bell peppers and onions are softened. Add the vinegar, salt, and pepper, then turn off the heat.

6. Prepare the barbecue grill for direct cooking and preheat to medium-hot. Lightly brush the grill rack with oil and cook the sausages for 6 minutes on each side, or until the center of the meat is no longer pink and the juices run clear.

7. Slice the sub rolls down the middle, fill each with mayonnaise, one of the sausages, and the bell pepper mixture. Finish with some arugula and serve.

Pork Meatball Skewers
with Smoked Cheese Sauce

 SERVES 4

PREP: 30 MINS

 COOK: 20-25 MINS

INGREDIENTS

1 pound ground pork

2 tablespoons olive oil, plus extra for brushing

2 shallots, finely chopped

1 cup panko bread crumbs

½ cup milk

1 teaspoon fennel seeds

1 teaspoon dried oregano

1 extra-large egg, beaten

⅔ cup grated Parmesan cheese, plus extra to serve

1 teaspoon salt

1 teaspoon pepper

4 pickles, sliced

SMOKED CHEESE SAUCE

4 tablespoons butter

⅓ cup flour

2½ cups milk

1 tablespoon yellow mustard

1 cup shredded smoked cheese

½ teaspoon salt

½ teaspoon pepper

1. To make the meatballs, put the ground pork, oil, shallots, bread crumbs, milk, fennel seeds, oregano, beaten egg, Parmesan, salt, and pepper into a large bowl and mix well to combine. Divide the mixture into golf ball-size balls. Thread the balls onto four metal skewers.

2. Prepare the barbecue grill for direct cooking and preheat to medium-hot.

3. Meanwhile, make the cheese sauce by melting the butter in a medium saucepan over low heat. Add the flour and cook until a light golden brown.

4. In a small saucepan, bring the milk to a boil and then add it slowly to the butter mixture, stirring continuously with a wooden spoon to avoid any lumps. When all the milk has been added, add the mustard, cheese, salt, and pepper. Remove from the heat and set aside in a warm place.

5. Lightly brush the grill rack with oil and cook the skewers, with the lid on, for 10—12 minutes, turning every now and then. When the skewers are cooked through and the juices run clear, remove from the grill and serve with the cheese sauce, sliced pickles, and Parmesan.

IF YOU DON'T LIKE SMOKED
CHEESE, THIS RECIPE WILL ALSO
WORK WITH CHEDDAR OR ANY
BLUE CHEESE.

How to Achieve Maximum Flavor

Having a good-quality grill and knowing how to use it are, of course, key to grilling up a good barbecue, but there's more to it than just knowing how to light a fire or wield a pair of tongs. Here are our best hints and tips for achieving maximum flavor from your grill.

START WITH THE BEST
Always choose the freshest, highest-quality meat available. Better still, get to know your neighborhood butcher and ask him or her to make recommendations based on what's available.

PREP IT RIGHT
Before you even strike the first match, make sure your meat is prepped properly. Trim the excess fat, score the meat so that the flavors penetrate as deeply as possible, marinate the meat or coat it with a seasoning rub, and let it rest at room temperature for 30–60 minutes before placing it on the hot grill rack.

SEASON AT THE LAST MINUTE
Even if you marinate your meat in a mixture that contains salt, much of it is lost when you drain off the marinade. Add salt just before you place the meat on the grill rack to make sure that it is well-seasoned. If you are using a spice rub with adequate salt, this is not a concern.

LEAVE IT ALONE
Ideally you want your meat to have a nice seared crust. In order to achieve this, it is imperative that you back off. Place the meat on the grill rack and let it cook until deep, dark grill marks appear on the underside before you move the meat or flip it.

GIVE IT A REST
Letting meat rest for several minutes after cooking keeps it moist and juicy. Remove the meat from the grill and set it on a cutting board. Wait anywhere from 5 minutes (for thin steaks or chops) to 15–30 minutes (for a roast or whole chicken), then slice or carve as desired.

Lamb Chops
with Tomato-Mint Sauce

 SERVES 4

 PREP: 20 MINS + MARINATING

 COOK: 1-1¼ HOURS

INGREDIENTS

8 lamb loin chops or
4 lamb shoulder chops,
about ¾–1 inch thick

salt and pepper,
to taste

MARINADE

¼ cup olive oil

¼ cup red wine vinegar

2 garlic cloves,
finely chopped

TOMATO-MINT SAUCE

2 tablespoons olive oil

1 small onion, diced

8 plum tomatoes (about
1 pound), peeled,
seeded, and chopped

1–2 jalapeño chiles or
Thai chiles, seeded and
finely chopped

½ cup sugar

juice of 1 lemon

½ teaspoon salt

2 tablespoons chopped
fresh mint leaves, plus
extra to garnish

1. To make the marinade, combine the oil, vinegar, and garlic in a baking dish or bowl large enough to hold all of the chops. Season the chops with salt and pepper and add them to the marinade, turning to coat. Cover and let marinate in the refrigerator for 2–8 hours.

2. To make the sauce, heat the oil over medium-high heat in a large, heavy skillet. Add the onion and cook, stirring, for about 5 minutes, until it begins to soften. Add the tomatoes, chiles, sugar, lemon juice, and salt and bring to a boil. Reduce the heat to medium-low and simmer, stirring occasionally, for about 45 minutes, until the tomatoes have broken down and the sauce becomes thick. Stir in the mint, remove from the heat, and set aside.

3. Prepare the barbecue grill for direct cooking and preheat to hot. Place the chops on the grill rack and cook for 5–7 minutes on each side. Check that the center of the meat is no longer pink and the juices run clear.

4. Serve immediately with the tomato-mint sauce and garnish with mint leaves.

THE CHILES IN THIS SAUCE
GIVE THE LAMB CHOPS A SPICY
KICK—ADD MORE CHILES TO
TURN UP THE HEAT.

Lamb Burgers
with Tzatziki & Feta Cheese

 SERVES 4

 PREP: 15 MINS

 COOK: 10 MINS

INGREDIENTS

BURGERS

1 pound ground lamb

1 teaspoon salt

1 teaspoon pepper

1 teaspoon cumin seeds

TZATZIKI

¼ cup Greek yogurt

small bunch of fresh mint, chopped

small bunch of fresh dill, chopped

½ cucumber, sliced

½ teaspoon salt

½ teaspoon pepper

PICKLED ONION

1 red onion, sliced

2 tablespoons red wine vinegar

½ teaspoon salt

oil, for brushing

4 hamburger buns

⅔ cup crumbled feta cheese

1. To make the burgers, mix together the lamb, salt, pepper, and cumin seeds in a medium bowl.

2. Divide the meat mixture into four equal balls, then shape them into patties.

3. To make the tzatziki, mix all of the ingredients in a small bowl and stir to combine.

4. To make the pickled onion, mix together the onion, vinegar, and salt in another small bowl.

5. Prepare the barbecue grill for direct cooking and preheat to medium-hot.

6. Brush the grill rack with a little oil. Cook the patties for 5 minutes on each side, or until the center of the meat is no longer pink and the juices run clear.

7. Divide the burgers between the buns and top with the tzatziki, feta cheese, and pickled onions. Serve immediately.

THESE LAMB BURGERS MAKE
A GREAT ALTERNATIVE TO
TRADITIONAL HAMBURGERS OR
TURKEY BURGERS.

Lamb Kabobs

SERVES 4

PREP: 20 MINS

COOK: 10 MINS

INGREDIENTS

LAMB SKEWERS

2¼ pounds lamb shoulder, diced

2 tablespoons olive oil

1 teaspoon paprika

1 teaspoon dried oregano

1 teaspoon ground cumin

1 teaspoon dried thyme

1 teaspoon salt

1 teaspoon pepper

4 large flat breads

¼ cup Greek yogurt

1 large tomato, chopped

1 small red onion, sliced

1 cup shredded red cabbage

small bunch of fresh cilantro, chopped

2 lemons, halved

sriracha or other hot chili sauce

1. To make the lamb skewers, mix the lamb, oil, paprika, oregano, cumin, thyme, salt, and pepper in a medium bowl and stir to coat the lamb thoroughly.

2. Prepare the barbecue grill for direct cooking and preheat to hot.

3. Thread the lamb onto four metal skewers. Place on the grill rack and cook on all four sides for 2 minutes for medium-rare, or to your preference. Check that the center of the meat is no longer pink and the juices run clear. Let the lamb rest for a couple of minutes in a warm place.

4. Place the breads on the grill rack and cook on both sides for a few seconds until pliable.

5. Remove the lamb from the skewers. Spread the flat breads with the yogurt and top with lamb, tomato, onion, cabbage, and cilantro. Squeeze the lemons over the top and drizzle with chili sauce.

NAAN, AVAILABLE FROM
INDIAN GROCERS, IS A GREAT
ALTERNATIVE TO FLAT BREADS.
THEY NEED JUST A FEW SECONDS
MORE TO HEAT THROUGH.

Chapter 4
CHICKEN & TURKEY

Sticky Bourbon
Chicken Wings

SERVES 4

PREP: 20 MINS

COOK: 30 MINS

INGREDIENTS

2¼ pounds chicken wings, tips removed

oil, for brushing

RUB

1 tablespoon paprika

½ teaspoon ground cumin

1 teaspoon dried thyme

1 teaspoon dried oregano

1 teaspoon salt

1 teaspoon pepper

BOURBON GLAZE

2 tablespoons bourbon

2 tablespoons apple cider vinegar

1 tablespoon Worcestershire sauce

2 tablespoons molasses

2 tablespoons ketchup

2 tablespoons chipotle paste

1 tablespoon yellow mustard

½ teaspoon salt

½ teaspoon pepper

1. To make the rub, combine all of the ingredients together in a large bowl.

2. Cut each chicken wing in half. Add the wing pieces to the bowl containing the rub and turn until coated thoroughly.

3. To make the bourbon glaze, put a medium saucepan over medium heat. Add the bourbon and flambé. When the flames have died down, add the rest of the glaze ingredients and simmer over medium heat until the sauce has reduced by half.

4. Prepare the barbecue grill for direct cooking and preheat to medium-hot.

5. Thread half of the chicken wing pieces onto two metal skewers, creating a raft shape. Repeat with the other half of the wings. Brush the wings with the bourbon glaze.

6. Brush the grill rack lightly with oil and cook the wings for 10 minutes on each side, brushing with more glaze as they cook.

7. When the wings are cooked, the meat should come easily away from the bone. Check that the juices run clear when the thickest part of the meat is pierced with a skewer and the center of the meat is no longer pink. Remove from the skewers and serve.

TRY MAKING A LARGER BATCH OF THE BOURBON GLAZE. IT WILL KEEP IN THE REFRIGERATOR FOR AT LEAST A MONTH AND CAN BE USED AS A CONDIMENT.

Cuts of chicken

NECK AND GIBLETS

Most people discard the chicken's neck and giblets (the heart, liver, and gizzard)—usually packed in the bird's cavity—but they can be used to make great stock.

WING

This is the boniest part of the chicken and when cooked on a barbecue grill, they turn crispy and delicious.

WISHBONE

When deboning a chicken, you will need to remove the wishbone by cutting through the meat at the neck cavity and taking out this bone.

WING TIP

These can be fried or used to make a tasty chicken stock.

THIGH

The thigh is sometimes sold without the bone and skin and is juicy and flavorful. It is dark meat and can contain more fat than the breast.

BREAST

This is a juicy, white meat cut that is versatile and has little fat. It is great when marinated and chargrilled, and can be sold with or without the skin.

DRUMSTICK

This dark meat cut is great when cooked in a sticky marinade and eaten with your fingers.

Cuts of turkey

WING TIP

These are often discarded but can be useful for making stock.

WING

Turkey wings are less popular than chicken wings, but they can be roasted or braised to create a crispy, tasty dish.

NECK AND GIBLETS

Most people discard turkey necks and giblets (the liver, heart, and gizzard)—usually packed in the bird's cavity—but they can be stewed in curries or Caribbean cuisine.

THIGH

The thigh stays more juicy during cooking if you keep the skin on. It has a higher fat content than breast, but has a deeper flavor.

WISHBONE

The wishbone is usually pulled apart by two people to celebrate at Christmas.

DRUMSTICK

The drumstick requires long and slow cooking but then it is tender and falls away from the bone.

BREAST

The turkey breast may be sold as a roast, without the legs and wings. It is great for roasting for people who prefer the taste of just white meat. Cutlets are also available.

Beer-Can Cajun Chicken

PREP: 20 MINS
+ MARINATING
+ RESTING

COOK:
1 HOUR

INGREDIENTS

1 medium whole chicken

1 large can of beer

CAYENNE RUB

2 tablespoons olive oil

2 teaspoons sweet smoked paprika

1 tablespoon packed light brown sugar

1 teaspoon oregano

1 teaspoon dried thyme

1 teaspoon garlic salt

1 teaspoon onion powder

½ teaspoon cayenne pepper

½ teaspoon salt

1 teaspoon pepper

1. Combine all the rub ingredients together in a medium bowl big enough to fit the chicken in. Add the chicken and massage the rub all over the inside and outside of the chicken. Cover and put into the refrigerator for at least a couple of hours.

2. Remove the chicken from the refrigerator at least an hour before you want to cook it, so it reaches room temperature.

3. Prepare the barbecue grill for indirect cooking and preheat to medium-hot.

4. Open the can of beer, remove half of the contents, and then put the can in a beer can chicken roaster (or see tip on right).

5. Place the chicken over the beer can, inserting the can all the way into the cavity.

6. Cook the chicken on the grill rack with the lid on for 1 hour, or until the juices run clear when the thickest part of the meat is pierced with the tip of a sharp knife and the center of the meat is no longer pink.

7. Cover with aluminum foil and let rest for 15 minutes in a warm place before serving.

IF YOU DON'T HAVE A BEER CAN
CHICKEN ROASTER, JUST BE
CAREFUL WHEN PLACING ON
THE BARBECUE TO AVOID THE
CHICKEN FALLING OVER.

BBQ Chicken
with Lemon Butter

 ☆ SERVES 4–6 ☆

PREP: 20 MINS

COOK: 30–40 MINS

INGREDIENTS

1 whole chicken, about 3½ pounds

LEMON BUTTER

1 stick butter, softened

3 garlic cloves, finely chopped

1 tablespoon chopped fresh oregano

1 teaspoon salt

½ teaspoon pepper

zest and juice of 1 lemon

1. To make the lemon butter, put all the ingredients into a small bowl and mix with a fork until well combined.

2. Prepare the barbecue grill for direct cooking and preheat to medium-hot.

3. Butterfly the chicken by using kitchen shears to cut along both sides of the backbone to remove it. Next, remove the breastbone that runs down the middle of the breast. Trim off any excess skin and fat.

4. Slide your fingers gently under the skin of the breast and legs to separate it from the meat. Spread 2–3 tablespoons of the butter mixture under the skin. Spread about 1 tablespoon over the outside.

5. Place the chicken on the grill rack, breast side up, and cook for 10 minutes. Baste with more of the butter mixture, turn the chicken breast side down, and continue to cook, turning and basting every 10 minutes, for a total cooking time of 30–40 minutes. Check that the juices run clear when the thickest part of the meat is pierced with the tip of a sharp knife and the center of the meat is no longer pink.

6. Carve and serve immediately.

1

4

5

BUTTERFLYING, OR FLATTENING,
A CHICKEN HELPS IT
COOK QUICKLY AND EVENLY
SO IT DOESN'T DRY OUT
DURING COOKING.

BBQ Chicken Wings

SERVES 4

PREP: 20 MINS + MARINATING

COOK: 20 MINS

INGREDIENTS

2¼ pounds chicken wings, tips removed

oil, for brushing

BBQ MARINADE

1 tablespoon paprika

2 tablespoons olive oil

2 tablespoons ketchup

2 tablespoons yellow mustard

2 tablespoons maple syrup

1 tablespoon Worcestershire sauce

1. To make the marinade, mix together all the ingredients in a large bowl. Add the chicken wings and use your hands to mix and coat thoroughly in the marinade.

2. Cover the bowl with plastic wrap and put into the refrigerator for at least 2 hours.

3. Remove the chicken wings from the refrigerator at least an hour before you want to cook them, so they reach room temperature.

4. Prepare the barbecue grill for direct cooking and preheat to medium-hot.

5. Lightly brush the grill rack with oil. Cook the chicken wings for 10 minutes on both sides, or until they are caramelized, slightly charred, and the meat comes easily away from the bone. Check that the juices run clear when the thickest part of the meat is pierced with the tip of a sharp knife and the center of the meat is no longer pink, then serve immediately.

CHICKEN WING TIPS CAN
BE SAVED AND USED TO
MAKE STOCK.

Chicken Thighs
with Caesar Marinade

SERVES 4

PREP: 20 MINS
+ MARINATING

COOK:
20 MINS

INGREDIENTS

2¼ pounds chicken thighs, skin removed

oil, for brushing

CAESAR MARINADE

4 salted anchovies, chopped

2 garlic cloves, crushed

⅔ cup finely grated Parmesan cheese

3 tablespoons mayonnaise

1 tablespoon Worcestershire sauce

small bunch of fresh thyme, chopped

juice and zest of 1 lemon

1 teaspoon salt

1 teaspoon pepper

1. To make the marinade, put all the marinade ingredients into a nonmetallic dish big enough to fit the chicken thighs in. Add the chicken, turning a few times to coat thoroughly. Cover with plastic wrap and put into the refrigerator for at least 2 hours.

2. Remove the chicken from the refrigerator at least an hour before you want to cook it, so it can reach room temperature.

3. Prepare the barbecue grill for direct cooking and preheat to medium-hot.

4. Lightly brush the grill rack with oil. Place the chicken thighs on the grill rack and cook for 10 minutes on both sides. Check the chicken is cooked by seeing that the juices run clear when the thickest part of the meat is pierced with the tip of a sharp knife and the center of the meat is no longer pink. Slice and serve immediately.

THIS MARINADE HAS ALL THE FLAVOR OF A CAESAR SALAD BUT WITH NONE OF THE LETTUCE!

Chicken Drumsticks
with Satay Glaze

 ⭐ SERVES 4 ⭐

 PREP: 20 MINS + MARINATING

 COOK: 25 MINS

INGREDIENTS

2¼ pounds chicken drumsticks

SOY MARINADE

2 tablespoons light soy sauce

2 tablespoons packed light brown sugar

1 teaspoon turmeric

1 tablespoon sesame oil

1 tablespoon vegetable oil

SATAY GLAZE

⅔ cup coconut cream or coconut milk

2 tablespoons peanut butter

1 tablespoon sriracha chili sauce

2 tablespoons packed light brown sugar

1 teaspoon Thai fish sauce

1. To make the marinade, put all of the marinade ingredients into a nonmetallic dish big enough to fit the chicken in. Add the chicken, turning a few times to coat thoroughly. Cover with plastic wrap and put into the refrigerator for at least 2 hours.

2. Remove the chicken from the refrigerator at least an hour before you want to cook it, so that it can reach room temperature.

3. To make the satay glaze, put all the ingredients into a small saucepan and stir with a wooden spoon until well combined. Cook for 5 minutes, or until slightly syrupy.

4. Prepare the barbecue grill for direct cooking and preheat to medium.

5. Place the chicken on the grill rack and cook the drumsticks for 20 minutes, turning every now and then and basting with the satay glaze.

6. Check the chicken is cooked by seeing that the juices run clear when the thickest part of the meat is pierced with the tip of a sharp knife and the center of the meat is no longer pink. Glaze one last time and serve.

IF YOU HAVE ANY LEFTOVER GLAZE, IT'S GREAT IN A NOODLE SALAD, WITH SHRIMP, CHICKEN, AND BASIL.

Ancho Chile & Cola Chicken

SERVES 4

PREP: 20 MINS + MARINATING

COOK: 45 MINS

INGREDIENTS

4 chicken breasts, skin on

PAPRIKA MARINADE

¼ cup olive oil

1 teaspoon dried thyme

1 tablespoon paprika

1 tablespoon packed light brown sugar

1 tablespoon ground cumin

1 teaspoon salt

1 teaspoon pepper

ANCHO CHILI SAUCE

2 dried ancho chiles, coarsely chopped and stems removed

1 teaspoon dried oregano

1⅓ cups cola

½ cup molasses

1 teaspoon vanilla extract

1 (14½-ounce) can plum or roma tomatoes

⅔ cup apple cider vinegar

1. To make the marinade, put all the marinade ingredients into a nonmetallic dish big enough to fit the chicken in. Add the chicken, turning a few times to coat thoroughly. Cover with plastic wrap and put into the refrigerator for at least 2 hours.

2. Remove the chicken from the refrigerator at least an hour before you want to cook it, so it can reach room temperature.

3. To make the sauce, put all the sauce ingredients into a medium saucepan and cook over low heat for 30 minutes, or until the sauce has reduced by half. Stir every now and then.

4. When the sauce is ready, remove from the heat and let cool slightly. Blend thoroughly with a handheld blender.

5. Prepare the barbecue grill for direct cooking and preheat to medium-hot.

6. Place the chicken, skin side down, on the grill rack for 6 minutes, then turn over and cook for another 6 minutes. Check the chicken is cooked by seeing that the juices run clear when the thickest part of the meat is pierced with the tip of a sharp knife and the center of the meat is no longer pink. Let the chicken rest in a warm place for a couple of minutes before serving with the sauce.

FOR A SUPERSPICY SAUCE,
TRY ADDING A FEW HABANERO
CHILES AS WELL.

Buttermilk BBQ Chicken

SERVES 4

PREP: 20 MINS
+ MARINATING
+ RESTING

COOK:
25 MINS

INGREDIENTS

2 small chickens

BUTTERMILK MARINADE

1¼ cups buttermilk

2 tablespoons olive oil

2 teaspoons paprika

1 teaspoon garlic salt

1 teaspoon celery salt

1 teaspoon onion powder

1 teaspoon dried oregano

1 teaspoon crushed red pepper flakes

1 teaspoon pepper

1. Cut the chickens in half by removing the backbone, then cut through the breastbone. Score the chickens on the flesh side, which will help speed up the cooking process.

2. To make the marinade, mix together all the ingredients in a large bowl. Add the chicken halves and mix well until the chicken is well coated. Cover the bowl with plastic wrap and let marinate in the refrigerator for 2 hours.

3. Remove the chicken halves from the refrigerator at least an hour before you want to cook them, so they can reach room temperature.

4. Prepare the barbecue grill for direct cooking and preheat to medium-hot.

5. Place the chicken halves, skin side up, on the grill rack and cook, with a lid on, for 15 minutes. Turn the chicken over and cook for an additional 10 minutes. Make sure the chicken is cooked by checking the juices run clear when the thickest part of the meat is pierced with the tip of a sharp knife and the center of the meat is no longer pink. Let the chicken rest in a warm place for 5 minutes before serving.

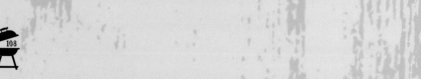

THIS RECIPE WORKS WELL
FOR MAKING SOUTHERN FRIED
CHICKEN. JUST COAT IN SEASONED
FLOUR AND DEEP-FRY FOR
15 MINUTES.

Whole Roasted Chicken
with Jerk Spices

SERVES 4

PREP: 20 MINS
+ MARINATING
+ RESTING

COOK:
1 HOUR

INGREDIENTS

1 medium whole chicken

lime wedges and hot
chili sauce, to serve

JERK MARINADE

1 tablespoon allspice

3 cloves

4 scallions

1 garlic clove

small bunch of
fresh thyme

1 Scotch bonnet chile

small bunch of fresh
cilantro

2 tablespoons apple
cider vinegar

juice of 1 lime

zest and juice of
1 clementine

3 tablespoons honey

1 teaspoon salt

1 teaspoon pepper

1. To make the marinade, put all the ingredients into a food processor and blend until smooth. You may need to scrape down the sides of the bowl a few times.

2. Put the chicken into a large bowl and pour the marinade over the chicken. Using your hands, rub the marinade all over the inside and outside of the chicken. Cover with plastic wrap and let rest in the refrigerator for 2 hours.

3. Remove the chicken from the refrigerator at least an hour before you want to cook it, so it can reach room temperature. Put the chicken into a deep roasting pan, then add a small amount of water to the pan.

4. Prepare the barbecue grill for indirect cooking and preheat to medium.

5. Place the roasting pan in the center of the grill rack, with the lid on, and cook for 1 hour, or until the juices run clear when the thickest part of the chicken is pierced with the tip of a sharp knife and the center of the meat is no longer pink.

6. Let the chicken rest in a warm place for 5 minutes, then serve with lime wedges and chili sauce.

YOU CAN ALSO TRY THIS
MARINADE WITH A MEATY FISH,
SUCH AS RED SNAPPER, BASS,
OR SALMON.

Honey & Orange
Turkey Breast

 SERVES 4

PREP: 30 MINS
+ BRINING
+ RESTING

COOK:
6 HOURS

INGREDIENTS

6½-pound turkey breast roast, skin on

CRANBERRY MARINADE

10½ cups water

2 cups sea salt crystals

1 cup honey

zest and juice of 3 oranges

10 cloves

20 peppercorns

small bunch of fresh thyme, chopped

3 cinnamon sticks

10½ cups cranberry juice

1. To make the marinade, put 2 cups of the water into a large saucepan. Add the salt, honey, orange zest, orange juice, cloves, peppercorns, thyme, and cinnamon sticks. Bring to a boil until the salt has dissolved. Turn off the heat, then add the rest of the water. Add the cranberry juice and let cool completely.

2. Put the turkey roast into a large, nonmetallic container and pour the marinade over it. Put a plate on top to keep the turkey submerged. Cover and put in the refrigerator overnight.

3. Remove the turkey from the refrigerator at least an hour before you want to cook it, so it can reach room temperature.

4. Prepare the barbecue grill for smoking and preheat to low.

5. Place the turkey, skin side up, on the grill rack and cook, with a lid on, for 6 hours. Check the turkey is cooked by seeing that the juices run clear when the thickest part of the meat is pierced with the tip of a sharp knife and the center of the meat is no longer pink. Cover with aluminum foil and let rest for 30 minutes in a warm place before slicing and serving.

THIS SMOKED TURKEY TASTES
GREAT ON ITS OWN AND IT ALSO
MAKES AN AWESOME ADDITION TO
A SANDWICH OR SALAD.

Turkey Drumsticks
with Mexican Spice Rub

INGREDIENTS

4 turkey drumsticks,
about 1 pound each

MEXICAN RUB

2 tablespoons packed
light brown sugar

2 tablespoons olive oil

zest and juice of
1 orange

1 tablespoon salt

1 tablespoon paprika

1 teaspoon pepper

1 teaspoon garlic salt

1 tablespoon
chipotle puree

1 tablespoon
ground cumin

1 teaspoon dried oregano

1 teaspoon dried thyme

1. To make the rub, mix all of the ingredients together in a large bowl. Add the turkey drumsticks, turning a few times to coat thoroughly.

2. Cover with plastic wrap and put into the refrigerator for at least 2 hours. Remove the drumsticks from the refrigerator at least an hour before you want to cook them, so they can reach room temperature.

3. Prepare the barbecue grill for indirect cooking and preheat to medium.

4. Place the turkey on the grill rack and cook, with the lid on, for 40 minutes. Check the turkey is cooked by seeing that the juices run clear when the thickest part of the meat is pierced with the tip of a sharp knife and the center of the meat is no longer pink.

5. Cover with aluminum foil and let rest in a warm place before serving.

WET RUBS CAN BE MADE WELL IN
ADVANCE AND KEPT IN A JAR IN
THE REFRIGERATOR FOR UP
TO TWO WEEKS.

Chicken Teriyaki Skewers

SERVES 4

PREP: 20 MINS + MARINATING

COOK: 20 MINS

INGREDIENTS

1 pound skinless, boneless chicken thighs

2 tablespoons light soy sauce

1 tablespoon sesame oil

1 tablespoon vegetable oil, plus extra for brushing

1 bunch of scallions, cut into 2-inch pieces

TERIYAKI SAUCE

2 tablespoons light soy sauce

2 tablespoons mirin (Japanese rice wine) or sherry

1 tablespoon rice vinegar

1-inch piece of fresh ginger, sliced

¼ cup sugar

1. Cut the chicken into bite-size pieces and put into a nonmetallic bowl. Add the soy sauce and the oils and mix until the pieces are coated thoroughly.

2. Cover the bowl with plastic wrap and put into the refrigerator for at least 2 hours. Remove the chicken from the refrigerator at least an hour before you want to cook it, so it can reach room temperature.

3. To make the sauce, heat all of the ingredients in a small saucepan over medium heat until it is reduced by half and slightly syrupy. Remove from the heat and discard the ginger.

4. Prepare the barbecue grill for direct cooking and preheat to medium-hot.

5. Thread the chicken pieces and scallions onto four metal skewers.

6. Lightly brush the grill rack with oil and cook the skewers for 5 minutes on each side. Brush the chicken skewers with the teriyaki sauce while cooking.

7. Check the chicken is cooked and the center of the meat is no longer pink by cutting into the center of a piece. Brush the chicken pieces and scallions with the sauce one last time and serve.

ALWAYS WASH THE SCALLIONS
BEFORE USE TO REMOVE ANY
GRIT OR DIRT.

What's Going Wrong?

Five Common BBQ Mistakes and How to Fix Them

A true barbecue master makes grilling look easy, but there are plenty o
ways even a barbecue guru can screw it up. Here are the five most common
barbecue mistakes and some advice about what to do instead. Read up
before the weekend and you'll show them who's boss.

1. Using a dirty grill: There's no nice way to say this. A dirty grill is gross.
Your guests don't want to eat the remnants of last weekend's cookout. The
solution? Clean your grill every time you use it. You can use a metal brush
or a wadded-up piece of aluminium foil to scrape the nasty stuff off.

2. Your food tastes like lighter fluid: Lighter fluid is really helpful when you
light your coals. The problem is that it can often impart a foul taste to the
food you've worked so hard to prepare. The solution is surprisingly simple—skip
the lighter fluid. Either use a chimney starter, a cylindrical device that helps
get coals going without the need for lighter fluid, or use a gas grill instead of
charcoal. Simple as that.

3. Grilling too soon: If you don't adequately preheat the grill, you run the
risk of burning food on the outside before it cooks through. Allow for a minimum
of 10 minutes to heat up a gas grill and 30–40 minutes for a charcoal grill.

4. Food is undercooked or takes much longer than you expected: Undercooked food
isn't just unpleasant, it can be a real disaster if it makes you or one of your
guests sick. The key to cooking food to the proper temperature is to make sure
the heat is high enough on your grill and, if cooking with the lid closed, don't
open the lid more often than necessary. Every time you open the lid, you lose
enough heat that you'll need to add a minimum of about 5 more minutes to your
total cooking time.

5. Pressing on meat while it cooks: We know it's tempting to press down on meat,
especially burgers, while it's cooking so that you can hear the sizzle of the
liquid that drips down onto the hot coals. But doing so is a big barbecue no-no.
This one is kind of a no-brainer when you think about it: If you want juicy meat
or burgers, don't squeeze the juiciness out while they cook. Let the meat sit on
the grill rack without disturbing it until the underside is deeply marked with
grill marks. Flip once. Cook until done. You're welcome.

Bacon-Wrapped Chicken
Burger with Grilled Pineapple

SERVES 4

PREP: 20 MINS

COOK: 25 MINS

INGREDIENTS

8 smoked pancetta strips

4 skinless, boneless chicken breasts

oil, for brushing

1 small butterhead lettuce, shredded

4 hamburger buns

GRILLED PINEAPPLE

½ a medium pineapple

1 tablespoon raw brown sugar

1 teaspoon pepper

RUSSIAN DRESSING

3 tablespoons mayonnaise

1 tablespoon ketchup

1 tablespoon horseradish

2 teaspoons hot pepper sauce

1 tablespoon Worcestershire sauce

1 shallot, grated

1. Lay two strips of the pancetta next to each other on a cutting board. Place a chicken breast on top of the strips and wrap the pancetta all the way around the breast. Repeat with the other three breasts.

2. To make the grilled pineapple, peel the pineapple and cut into four thick slices. Remove the core, then sprinkle each slice on both sides with the sugar and pepper.

3. Prepare the barbecue grill for direct cooking and preheat to medium-hot.

4. To make the dressing, mix all the ingredients together in a bowl, then set aside.

5. Brush your grill rack with oil, then place the chicken breasts on the rack. Cook for 10 minutes on each side, or until the juices run clear when the thickest part of the meat is pierced with the tip of a sharp knife and the center of the meat is no longer pink. When the chicken is cooked, remove from the heat and let rest in a warm place for 4 minutes.

6. While you are waiting for the chicken to rest, grill the pineapple slices for 2 minutes on each side, or until caramelized.

7. Divide the chicken, pineapple slices, lettuce, and dressing among the hamburger buns and serve immediately.

THIS BURGER IS A REAL MIX OF GORGEOUS FLAVORS, WITH THE CHICKEN, BACON, AND PINEAPPLE ALL PACKING A PUNCH.

Turkey Skewers
with Avocado Salsa

 SERVES 4

 PREP: 20 MINS
+ MARINATING

 COOK: 5 MINS

INGREDIENTS

4 turkey cutlets, 4–5 ounces each

olive oil, for brushing

warm tortillas, to serve

MARINADE

juice of 1 orange

juice of 2 limes

2 garlic cloves, crushed

1 teaspoon paprika

½ teaspoon salt

½ teaspoon chili powder

½ teaspoon cumin seeds, crushed

¼ teaspoon pepper

¼ cup olive oil

AVOCADO SALSA

2 avocados, pitted, peeled, and finely diced

juice of 1 lime

1 small red onion, finely diced

1 tablespoon chopped fresh cilantro

salt

1. Halve the turkey cutlets horizontally to make eight thinner pieces. Put them between two sheets of plastic wrap and pound with a meat mallet until flattened to ½ inch thick. Slice into strips about 1½ inches wide and 2½ inches long. Place in a single layer in a shallow dish.

2. To make the marinade, whisk together all the ingredients in a small bowl, then pour it over the turkey. Cover with plastic wrap and let rest in the refrigerator to marinate for at least 4 hours or overnight. Remove the turkey from the refrigerator at least an hour before you want to cook it, so it can reach room temperature.

3. Prepare the barbecue grill for direct cooking and preheat to hot.

4. To make the salsa, carefully mix the ingredients together and let rest at room temperature so the flavors can develop.

5. Remove the turkey from the marinade and lightly brush with oil. Thread the turkey pieces concertina-style onto metal skewers. Brush the grill rack with oil. Grill for 2–2½ minutes on each side, or until the juices run clear when the thickest part of the meat is pierced with the tip of a sharp knife and the center is no longer pink.

6. Remove the turkey from the skewers and serve immediately with the avocado salsa and tortillas.

THE LIME-INFUSED AVOCADO SALSA IS A GREAT COMPLEMENT TO THE FLAVOR OF THE TURKEY SKEWERS.

Chapter 5
FISH & SEAFOOD

Whole Grilled Shrimp
in Maple & Sriracha Butter

 ★ SERVES 4 ★

 PREP: 15 MINS

 COOK: 10-15 MINS

INGREDIENTS

2¼ pounds whole,
large shrimp

MAPLE & SRIRACHA BUTTER

1¼ sticks butter

2 tablespoons
maple syrup

2 tablespoons
sriracha chili sauce

1 tablespoon
apple cider vinegar

½ teaspoon salt

½ teaspoon pepper

1. Prepare the barbecue grill for direct cooking and preheat to hot.

2. Thread half of the shrimp onto two metal skewers, creating a raft shape. This will make cooking the shrimp a lot easier. Repeat with the other half of the shrimp.

3. To make the flavored butter, melt the butter in a small saucepan over low heat. Add the maple syrup, chili sauce, vinegar, salt, and pepper and stir to combine. Remove from the heat and keep in a warm place.

4. Place the shrimp on the grill rack and cook for 3 minutes on both sides, or until cooked through and the shells have turned dark pink.

5. Once the shrimp are cooked, remove the skewers. Put the shrimp into a medium bowl and pour the butter over them. Mix well and serve immediately.

IF USING WOODEN SKEWERS, MAKE SURE YOU SOAK THEM FIRST FOR 30 MINUTES TO STOP THEM FROM BURNING.

Spice-Rubbed Salmon
with Cilantro Pesto

 SERVES 4

PREP: 20 MINS

 COOK: 8 MINS

INGREDIENTS

1 tablespoon cumin seeds

1 teaspoon coriander seeds

4 salmon steaks, about 6 ounces each, skin on

olive oil, for brushing

salt and pepper

CILANTRO PESTO

2 small garlic cloves

large bunch of fresh cilantro, large stems discarded

large bunch of fresh flat-leaf parsley, large stems discarded

3 scallions, white and light green parts only

1–2 jalapeño chiles or Thai chiles, seeded

½ cup olive oil

juice of 1 lemon

1 teaspoon salt

1. To make the pesto, chop the garlic in a food processor. Add the cilantro, parsley, scallions, and chiles and process until finely chopped. Add the oil, lemon juice, and salt and process until well combined. Set aside.

2. Prepare the barbecue grill for direct cooking and preheat to high.

3. Coarsely grind the cumin seeds and coriander seeds in an electric spice grinder or in a mortar with a pestle. Brush the fish on both sides with oil, season with salt and pepper, and coat lightly with the seed mixture.

4. Place the salmon on the grill rack, skin side down, and cook with the lid on for about 4 minutes. Turn the salmon over and cook on the other side for an additional 4 minutes, or until the fish is opaque and flaky when separated with a fork. Serve immediately, topped with the pesto.

SALMON MAKES A TASTY
ALTERNATIVE TO MEAT AT A
BARBECUE AND THESE SPICES
WORK PERFECTLY WITH
THE FISH.

Scallops
in Hot Soy Sauce

★ SERVES 2 ★

PREP: 20 MINS

COOK: 15 MINS

INGREDIENTS

12 large fresh scallops, cleaned and roes removed

1 teaspoon salt

1 teaspoon pepper

oil, for brushing

HOT SOY SAUCE

1 tablespoon oil

1 tablespoon sesame oil

1 garlic clove, chopped

2 tablespoons mirin (Japanese rice wine) or sherry

2 tablespoons light soy sauce

1 tablespoon sugar

1 tablespoon oyster sauce

1-inch piece of fresh ginger, cut into matchsticks

4 scallions, sliced

1 red Thai chile, sliced

1. To make the soy sauce, heat the oils in a small saucepan over medium heat. Add the garlic and cook for 30 seconds, then add the rice wine, soy sauce, sugar, and oyster sauce. Reduce by half, then add the ginger, scallions, and chile. Remove from the heat and set aside.

2. Prepare the barbecue grill for direct cooking and preheat to hot.

3. Thread the scallops onto four metal skewers and sprinkle the skewers with the salt and pepper.

4. Brush the grill rack with a little oil. Cook the scallops for 30 seconds on each side, or until the scallops are caramelized on the outside but still creamy in the middle.

5. Remove from the skewers and serve with the hot soy sauce.

WHENEVER POSSIBLE, BUY
HAND-DIVED SCALLOPS, BECAUSE
THIS METHOD HAS MUCH LESS OF
AN ENVIRONMENTAL IMPACT.

Grilled Trout Tacos

SERVES 2 — PREP: 20 MINS — COOK: 12 MINS

INGREDIENTS

1 small red onion, sliced into rings

1 red jalapeño chile, sliced

2 tablespoons red wine vinegar

½ teaspoon salt

2 whole trout, 12–14 ounces each, gutted and cleaned

2 tablespoons olive oil

1 teaspoon dried oregano

1 teaspoon cumin seeds

1 teaspoon paprika

½ teaspoon salt

½ teaspoon pepper

6 soft tacos or small tortillas

FILLINGS

1 ripe avocado, chopped

juice of ½ lime

2 tablespoons sour cream

¼ cup grated salted ricotta cheese

small bunch of fresh cilantro, finely chopped

lime wedges, to serve

1. Put the onion, chile, vinegar, and salt into a small bowl. Mix together with a spoon, then let rest to pickle slightly.

2. Score the trout on both sides to help speed up the cooking process.

3. In a shallow, nonmetallic dish large enough to hold the trout, mix together the oil, oregano, cumin seeds, paprika, salt, and pepper. Add the trout, turning a couple of times to coat thoroughly.

4. Start to prepare the fillings by putting the avocado into a small bowl. Squeeze the lime juice over it and set aside.

5. Prepare the barbecue grill for direct cooking and preheat to medium-hot.

6. Place the trout on the grill rack and cook for 5 minutes on both sides, or until the flesh comes easily away from the bone. Check that the fish is opaque and flaky when separated with a fork.

7. Let the trout cool slightly, then remove the flesh from the bone.

8. Heat the tacos for a few seconds on each side, until they become pliable. Divide the tacos between two plates, then top with the trout, sour cream, avocado, salted ricotta, and pickled onion mixture. Sprinkle each taco with the cilantro and then serve with the lime wedges.

1

3

6

GRILLED SALMON OR SEA BASS
WILL ALSO WORK WELL WITH
THIS RECIPE; YOU MAY NEED
TO ADJUST THE COOKING
TIMES SLIGHTLY.

Peppered Tuna Steaks
with Anchovy Mayo

 SERVES 4

 PREP: 25 MINS

 COOK: 2 MINS

INGREDIENTS

¼ cup olive oil

1 teaspoon salt

1 teaspoon pepper

4 tuna steaks, about 8 ounces each

lemon wedges, to serve

ANCHOVY MAYO

1 egg yolk

splash of water

4 anchovy fillets

1 garlic clove, crushed

2 teaspoons Dijon mustard

1 cup canola oil

1 tablespoon white wine vinegar

salt and pepper

1. To make the mayo, put the egg yolk, water, anchovy fillets, garlic, and Dijon mustard into a food processor and process for 30 seconds, or until everything has doubled in volume. With the motor still running, start to add the oil slowly. When all of the oil has been added and the mayonnaise has thickened, season with salt and pepper, then add the vinegar. Transfer the mayo to a small bowl.

2. Prepare the barbecue grill for direct cooking and preheat to hot.

3. Put the olive oil, salt, and pepper into a nonmetallic dish large enough to hold all of the tuna steaks. Add the tuna, turning a few times to coat thoroughly.

4. Place the tuna on the grill rack and cook for 1 minute on each side for rare, or to your preference. Serve with the mayo and lemon wedges.

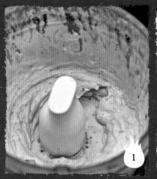

HOMEMADE MAYONNAISE IS
AMAZING BUT, IF YOU REALLY
DON'T HAVE THE TIME, STORE
BOUGHT WILL DO JUST FINE.

Squid
with Burned Corn Salsa

SERVES 4

PREP: 15 MINS + MARINATING

COOK: 12 MINS

INGREDIENTS

4 squid, about 8 ounces each, cleaned and gutted

SPICY MARINADE

¼ cup olive oil

1 teaspoon salt

1 teaspoon pepper

1 tablespoon paprika

1 tablespoon cumin

juice of 1 lemon

½ red onion, chopped

1 green jalapeño chile, chopped

small bunch of fresh cilantro, chopped

BURNED CORN SALSA

2 ears of corn

1 large tomato, chopped

1 small red onion, minced

small bunch of fresh cilantro, chopped

1 teaspoon crushed red pepper flakes

2 tablespoons extra virgin olive oil

1 tablespoon red wine vinegar

1 teaspoon salt

1 teaspoon pepper

1. To make the marinade for the squid, mix together all the ingredients in a nonmetallic bowl large enough to hold the squid. Add the squid and turn to coat thoroughly. Let marinate for 20 minutes.

2. Prepare the barbecue grill for direct cooking and preheat to hot.

3. To make the salsa, place the corn on the grill rack and cook until the corn is fairly charred all over. Remove and let cool. Keep the barbecue going.

4. Cut the kernels from the corn. Put the kernels into a medium bowl with all of the other salsa ingredients and mix well. Let rest for the flavors to mingle while you cook the squid.

5. Place the squid (and tentacles if there are any) on the grill rack and cook for 3 minutes on each side, or until the squid is nicely charred and has formed a cylindrical shape.

6. Slice the squid into rings and serve with the salsa.

TRY NOT TO OVERCOOK YOUR
SQUID, BECAUSE DOING SO WILL
MAKE IT CHEWY.

Grilled Lobster
with Nam Jim Sauce

★ SERVES 2 ★

PREP: 25 MINS
+ FREEZING

COOK: 20 MINS

INGREDIENTS

2 whole live lobsters, each about 1½ pounds

4 tablespoons salted butter, melted

1 teaspoon pepper

NAM JIM SAUCE

small bunch of fresh cilantro

10 green Thai chiles

½ teaspoon salt

¼ cup palm sugar or brown sugar

juice of 4 limes

1. Put the lobsters into the freezer for 2 hours before cooking. Bring a large saucepan of salted water to a boil and add the lobsters. Blanch for 5 minutes, then remove and put into iced water for 10 minutes.

2. Cut the lobsters in half lengthwise and remove the stomach sack at the head of the lobster. If there is one, remove the black line from the tail of the lobster and any roe in the head area. Crack the claws; this will let heat in when cooking.

3. Prepare the barbecue grill for direct cooking and preheat to medium-hot.

4. To make the nam jim sauce, put the cilantro, chiles, and salt into a food processor. Blend for 30 seconds, then scrape down the sides with a spatula to avoid any lumps. With the motor running, add the palm sugar and lime juice and blend until smooth. Put the sauce into a small bowl.

5. Brush the flesh side of the lobsters with the melted butter and sprinkle with pepper. Place the lobsters, flesh side down, on the grill rack and cook for 5 minutes. Turn over and cook for another 5 minutes, brushing with butter again. When the lobsters are cooked through, serve the nam jim sauce alongside for dipping.

1

2

5

BLANCHING THE LOBSTERS WILL
PREVENT ANY UNPLEASANT
SURPRISE OF UNCOOKED CLAW MEAT
ONCE YOU HAVE BARBECUED THEM.

Clams with Smoked Bacon

 SERVES 2

 PREP: 15 MINS + SOAKING

 COOK: 15 MINS

INGREDIENTS

2¼ pounds fresh clams, scrubbed

SMOKED BACON BUTTER

1¾ sticks butter

2 shallots, finely diced

2 garlic cloves, finely chopped

4 ounces smoked bacon, chopped

juice of 1 lemon

small bunch of fresh flat-leaf parsley, chopped

1. Soak the clams in fresh water for at least an hour before cooking, then remove from the water and drain well. Discard any clams with broken shells and any that refuse to close when tapped.

2. Prepare the barbecue grill for direct cooking and preheat to hot.

3. Melt the butter in a large skillet over medium heat. Add the shallots, garlic, and smoked bacon and cook for 8—10 minutes, or until browned. Remove from the heat and add the lemon and parsley. Set aside in a warm place.

4. Place the clams on the grill rack and cook for 4—5 minutes, or until the clams have fully opened. Discard any clams that have not opened.

5. Mix the cooked clams in the bacon butter and serve immediately.

FOR THOSE OF YOU WHO LIKE
THINGS A LITTLE SPICIER, TRY
ADDING A TABLESPOON OF CURRY
POWDER TO THE BACON BUTTER.

BBQ Shrimp Skewers

★ SERVES 4 ★

PREP: 15 MINS
+ MARINATING

COOK:
10 MINS

INGREDIENTS

1½ pounds shrimp, peeled and deveined

2 tablespoons olive oil

juice of 1 lime

1 garlic clove, finely chopped

1 teaspoon salt

¼–½ teaspoon ground chipotle or smoked paprika

Classic BBQ Sauce (see page 166), for brushing, plus extra to serve

lime halves, to serve

1. Put the shrimp into a large bowl and drizzle with the oil and lime juice. Add the garlic, salt, and ground chipotle and stir to coat well. Cover and chill in the refrigerator for 15 minutes.

2. Prepare the barbecue grill for direct cooking and preheat to hot.

3. Remove the shrimp from the marinade, discarding the marinade, and thread onto metal skewers (three to five shrimp per skewer, depending on the size of the shrimp).

4. Brush the shrimp on both sides with a little barbecue sauce, place on the grill rack, and cook for about 5 minutes on each side, brushing with some more sauce from time to time, or until the shrimp have cooked through, turned pink, and are slightly charred around the edges. Serve immediately with lime halves and barbecue sauce for dipping.

1   3   4

PLUMP, JUICY SHRIMP ARE
A PERFECT PARTNER FOR
THE CLASSIC SWEET-SPICY
BARBECUE SAUCE.

Chapter 6
VEGETABLES

Cheddar & Dill Pickle
Stuffed Potatoes

 **SERVES 4**

 PREP: 20 MINS

 COOK: 1 HOUR 10 MINS

INGREDIENTS

4 large russet or other baking potatoes

¼ cup olive oil

1 teaspoon salt

CHEDDAR & PICKLE FILLING

2 tablespoons sour cream

1 small red onion, chopped

1 cup shredded sharp cheddar cheese

⅓ cup chopped dill pickles

½ teaspoon salt

1 teaspoon pepper

1. Prepare the barbecue grill for indirect cooking and preheat to medium.

2. Put the baking potatoes into a baking pan. Drizzle with the oil and sprinkle with the salt.

3. Place on the grill rack, with the lid on, for an hour, or until the potatoes are soft to the touch. Remove from the grill and let cool slightly.

4. Cut the potatoes into halves and scoop out the flesh. Put the flesh into a bowl and mash lightly. Now add the filling ingredients and mix well with a wooden spoon.

5. Divide the mixture among the potato skins and then put back in the baking pan. Place on the grill rack and cook, with the lid on, for 10 minutes, or until lightly golden and bubbling. Serve immediately.

TRY EXPERIMENTING WITH
DIFFERENT CHEESES, SUCH
AS A BLUE CHEESE.

Seven Totally Unnecessary BBQ Tools You Won't Want to Be Without

1. Steam-Powered Grill Cleaning Tool

Fill this fancy-looking grill brush with water and the heat from the grill turns it into steam that powers grit and grime off your grate. There are several models available that include ergonomic handles, powerful stainless steel bristles, and built-in scrapers.

2. Burger Press

This handy gadget makes it easy to turn out perfectly consistent burger patties. Many models are adjustable, letting you set them for quarter-pound or half-pound burgers. They even add that all-important dimple that keeps it from shrinking up too much and bulging in the center.

3. Himalayan Salt Plate

A slab of pink salt from the Himalayas can be heated on a grill and used to cook seafood or meat. The salt retains heat and cooks evenly—and it adds complex flavor to the food at the same time.

4. Turner Tongs

Shaped liked spatulas and assembled like tongs, this tool helps you flip foods on the grill with ease. They are especially useful for delicate foods, such as fish.

5. Vegetable Grill Clips

Vegetable grill clips provide an easy way to grill veggies. Designed like a giant stainless steel clothespin, they grip veggie sticks and slices so that you can turn them easily on the grill. Most versions come in sets of four, making it easy to cook individual portions.

6. Wireless Food Thermometer

A wireless thermometer is the ultimate grilling gadget, letting you keep tabs on your food while also attending to your guests. Simple versions include a probe that goes into the meat and sends a signal to a receiver, or even your phone, computer, or tablet via Bluetooth, to let you know when the meat reaches your desired temperature.

7. Barbecue Tool Belt

Now that you have all these cool barbecue gadgets, where are you going to keep them all? A barbecue tool belt, of course. Designed to mimic the traditional carpenter's tool belt, these handy wearable organizers provide places to store everything from your turner tongs to your wireless thermometer receiver. And you'll look supercool with it on, too.

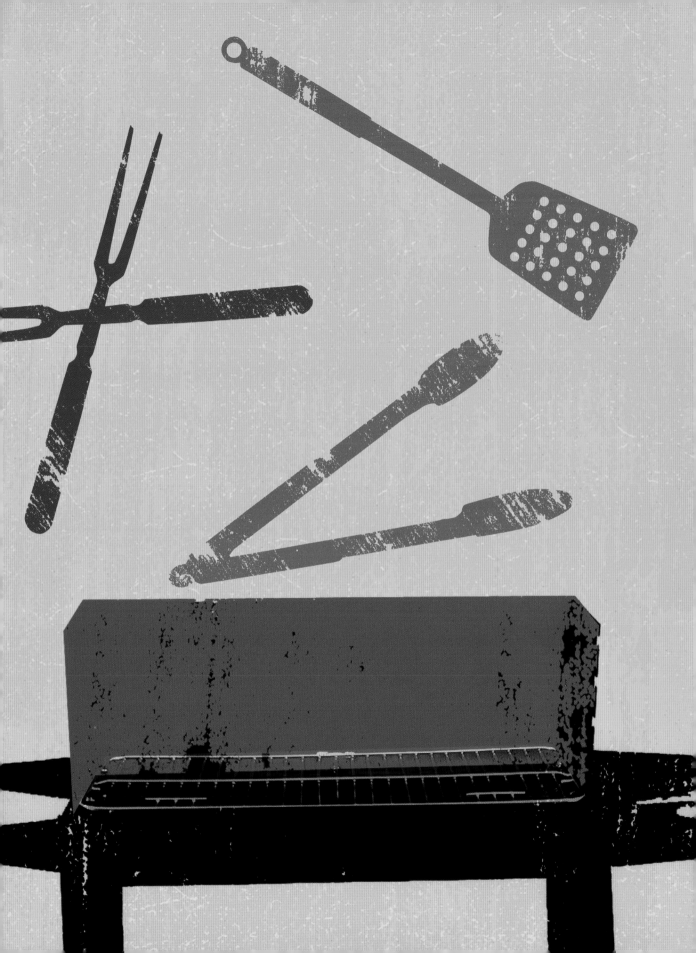

Satay Tofu Salad

SERVES 4

PREP: 20 MINS + MARINATING

COOK: 20 MINS

INGREDIENTS

1¾ pounds extra-firm tofu

MARINADE

2 tablespoons soy sauce

2 tablespoons sesame oil

2 tablespoons mirin (Japanese rice wine) or sherry

SATAY SAUCE

⅓ cup smooth peanut butter

½ cup coconut milk

2 tablespoons soy sauce

2 tablespoons packed light brown sugar

2 tablespoons hot water, plus extra if needed

juice of 1 lime

2 teaspoons chili paste, plus extra to taste

1 garlic clove, finely ground

1 tablespoon grated fresh ginger

TO SERVE

lettuce leaves

red and orange bell pepper strips

cucumber strips

whole basil leaves

1. Slice the tofu into 1-inch-thick slabs and pat dry with paper towels, pressing to release the excess moisture.

2. To make the marinade, combine the soy sauce, oil, and mirin in a large bowl. Add the tofu and turn to coat. Marinate for at least 30 minutes and up to 8 hours (refrigerate if marinating for longer than 30 minutes).

3. To make the satay sauce, combine the peanut butter, coconut milk, soy sauce, sugar, water, lime juice, chili paste, garlic, and ginger in a bowl and stir to mix well. Add more water, a teaspoon or two at a time, if needed, to reach the desired consistency.

4. Prepare the barbecue grill for direct cooking and preheat to medium-hot. Baste the tofu with some satay sauce, place on the grill rack, and cook for about 10 minutes on each side, or until golden brown. Cut into strips.

5. Serve the tofu on a bed of lettuce leaves, with the bell pepper and cucumber strips and basil leaves. Serve immediately with extra satay sauce for drizzling.

THIS TOFU SALAD IS A GREAT
ADDITION TO THE BARBECUE
FOR ANY VEGETARIAN GUESTS
OR FOR ANYONE ON A DIET.

Grilled Stuffed Bell Peppers

SERVES 4

PREP: 20 MINS

COOK: 35-40 MINS

INGREDIENTS

4 large red bell peppers

FILLING

2 tablespoons olive oil

1 small onion, diced

2 zucchini, diced

1 teaspoon salt

1 teaspoon ground cumin

1 (15-ounce) can chickpeas, drained and rinsed

1 cup freshly cooked brown rice

zest and juice of 1 lemon

2 tablespoons finely chopped fresh mint

⅔ cup crumbled feta cheese

1. Prepare the barbecue grill for indirect cooking and preheat to medium.

2. To make the filling, heat the oil in a heavy skillet over medium-high heat. Add the onion, zucchini, and salt and cook for about 5 minutes, stirring occasionally, until the onion is translucent and the zucchini are beginning to brown. Stir in the cumin and chickpeas and cook, stirring, for an additional 1 minute. Remove from the heat and let cool for a few minutes.

3. Combine the zucchini-and-chickpea mixture in a large bowl with the rice, lemon zest and juice, mint, and cheese. Stir to mix well.

4. Carefully slice off the tops of the red bell peppers, then core and seed them. Stuff them with the rice mixture, then replace the tops and secure them with toothpicks.

5. Place the stuffed peppers on the grill rack on their sides and cook, covered, for 25—30 minutes, turning every 5 minutes, until soft and just beginning to char. Serve immediately.

THIS TASTY DISH WILL DELIGHT
BOTH MEAT EATERS AND
VEGETARIANS ALIKE.

Stuffed Mushrooms

 SERVES 4

  PREP: 15 MINS COOK: 5 MINS

INGREDIENTS

2¼ pounds portobello mushrooms

⅓ cup olive oil

1 teaspoon salt

1 teaspoon pepper

4 garlic cloves, chopped

small bunch of fresh parsley, chopped

1 pound Gorgonzola or other blue cheese, sliced

1. Prepare the barbecue grill for direct cooking and preheat to hot.

2. Remove and discard the stems from the mushrooms. Drizzle the mushrooms with the olive oil, then sprinkle with the salt and pepper.

3. Add the garlic and parsley, and top the mushrooms with the cheese slices.

4. Place on the grill rack and cook, cheese side up, with the lid on for 5 minutes, or until the mushrooms are cooked and the cheese has melted.

THESE CAN BE MADE IN
ADVANCE AND KEPT IN THE
REFRIGERATOR FOR UP TO A DAY.

Grilled Cajun Vegetables
with Parmesan Grits

 ★ SERVES 4 ★

 PREP: 20 MINS

 COOK: 30 MINS

INGREDIENTS

¼ cup olive oil

1 teaspoon salt

1 tablespoon Cajun spice

2 zucchini, halved lengthwise

1 eggplant, quartered lengthwise

6 baby corn

1 red bell pepper, sliced

1 yellow bell pepper, sliced

¼ cup grated Parmesan cheese

GRITS

4 cups milk

4 tablespoons butter

2 cups instant grits

1 cup grated Parmesan cheese

1 teaspoon salt

1 teaspoon pepper

1. To make the grits, put the milk and butter into a heavy, stainless steel saucepan and warm over medium heat. When the milk and butter have started to boil, whisk in all the grits. Turn down the heat and stir with a wooden spoon for 10 minutes, or until the grits resembles a light mashed potatoes consistency. Remove from the heat, beat in the Parmesan, and sprinkle with the salt and pepper. Cover and let rest in a warm place.

2. Prepare the barbecue grill for direct cooking and preheat to medium-hot.

3. In a large bowl, mix together the oil, salt, and Cajun spice. Add the zucchini, eggplant, baby corn, and bell peppers and mix well to coat thoroughly.

4. Cook the vegetables on the grill rack for 4 minutes on each side, or until slightly charred but soft to the touch. Serve the vegetables over the grits, sprinkled with the Parmesan.

TRY USING GRITS AS AN
ALTERATIVE TO MASHED
POTATOES—IT'S GREAT WITH
BUTTER, CREAM, CHEESE,
AND HERBS.

Baked Sweet Potatoes
with Salsa

 SERVES 4

 PREP: 20 MINS

 COOK: 1 HOUR

INGREDIENTS

4 large sweet potatoes, about 12 ounces each

1 tablespoon olive oil, for rubbing

large pat of butter

2 tablespoons chopped fresh cilantro

½ cup crumbled feta cheese or other salty white cheese

salt and pepper, to taste

SALSA

3 tomatoes, seeded and finely diced

1 small red onion, finely diced

½–1 small green chile, seeded and finely diced

3 tablespoons chopped fresh cilantro

juice of 1 lime

1. Prepare the barbecue grill for indirect cooking and preheat to medium. Use some paper towels to rub the potatoes with a little olive oil and sprinkle with salt to coat lightly.

2. Tightly wrap the potatoes in pieces of double-thickness aluminum foil and place on the grill rack for about 1 hour.

3. Meanwhile, combine the salsa ingredients in a bowl. Add a little salt to taste. Let stand at room temperature to let the flavors develop.

4. When the potatoes are cooked, cut them open, fork the flesh to fluff up, and mix in a little butter, salt, and pepper, and most of the cilantro. Sprinkle with the cheese and the remaining cilantro. Serve immediately with the salsa spooned over the top.

SWEET POTATOES MAKE A TASTY
ALTERNATIVE TO NORMAL
BAKED POTATOES AND CONTAIN
LESS CARBS.

Mediterranean
Grilled Eggplants

★ SERVES 4 ★

PREP: 15 MINS

COOK: 15 MINS

INGREDIENTS

GRILLED EGGPLANTS

2 extra-large eggplants

¼ cup olive oil

1 teaspoon salt

1 teaspoon pepper

TAHINI YOGURT

2 tablespoons Greek yogurt

1 tablespoon tahini

1 garlic clove, crushed

juice of 1 lemon

salt and pepper, to taste

2 tablespoons butter

⅔ cup pine nuts

handful of arugula

⅔ cup raisins

2 tablespoons extra virgin olive oil, for drizzling

1. Cut the eggplants in half lengthwise, then score the flesh on a slight angle into diamond shapes.

2. Drizzle the eggplants with the olive oil and sprinkle with the salt and pepper.

3. Prepare the barbecue grill for direct cooking and preheat to medium-hot.

4. To make the yogurt, mix together the yogurt, tahini, garlic, and lemon juice in a small bowl. Season with salt and pepper.

5. Lay the eggplants on the grill rack, skin side down, and cook for 7 minutes, or until the flesh is golden and soft to the touch. Turn over and cook for another 7 minutes.

6. Meanwhile, heat the butter in a small skillet over medium heat. Add the pine nuts and toast until they are a light golden brown. When the eggplants are cooked, divide among four plates and serve with the tahini yogurt, arugula, pine nuts, and raisins. Drizzle with extra virgin olive oil and serve.

WHEN USING SALAD GREENS,
ALWAYS GIVE THEM A GOOD
SOAK IN WATER TO CLEAN AND
REVITALIZE THE LEAVES.

Squash & Cornmeal
Burgers

 ☆ SERVES 4-6 ☆

 PREP: 25 MINS + CHILLING

 COOK: 45-50 MINS

INGREDIENTS

½ butternut squash, peeled, seeded, and cut into chunks

⅔ cup water

½ cup instant cornmeal

1 cup grated celeriac

6 scallions, finely chopped

1 cup chopped pecans

⅔ cup freshly grated Parmesan cheese

2 tablespoons chopped fresh mixed herbs

2 tablespoons whole wheat flour

2 tablespoons sunflower oil, plus extra for oiling

salt and pepper, to taste

TO SERVE

hamburger buns

salad greens

tomato slices

ketchup

1. Cook the butternut squash in a saucepan of boiling water for 15—20 minutes, or until tender. Drain and finely chop or mash. Set aside.

2. Put the water into a separate saucepan and bring to a boil. Slowly pour in the cornmeal in a steady stream and cook over gentle heat, stirring, for 5—10 minutes, or according to package directions, until thick.

3. Remove the saucepan from the heat and stir in the butternut squash, celeriac, scallions, pecans, cheese, herbs, and salt and pepper to taste. Mix well, then shape into four to six patties. Coat the patties in the flour, cover and let chill for 1 hour.

4. Prepare the barbecue grill and preheat to medium-hot.

5. Grease the grill rack. Lightly brush the patties with the oil and cook for 5—6 minutes on each side, or until cooked through. Transfer to serving plates and serve immediately in the burger buns with the salad greens, tomato slices, and ketchup.

THESE DELICIOUS VEGGIE
BURGERS MAKE A GREAT
ALTERNATIVE TO THE STANDARD
BEAN BURGER.

Chapter 7
SIDES & SAUCES

Classic BBQ Sauce

MAKES 3¾ CUPS

PREP: 10 MINS

COOK: 50 MINS

INGREDIENTS

1 small onion

2 garlic cloves

1 tablespoon olive oil

1 cup ketchup

2 cups tomato puree or sauce

½ cup firmly packed light brown sugar

¼ cup apple cider vinegar

2 tablespoons Worcestershire sauce

½–1 teaspoon cayenne pepper

½–1 teaspoon smoked paprika or ground chipotle powder

1. Put the onion and garlic into a food processor and puree.

2. Heat the oil in a heavy skillet over medium-high heat. Add the onion-garlic puree and cook, stirring frequently, until it begins to brown.

3. Add the remaining ingredients and bring to a boil. Reduce the heat to medium and simmer for about 45 minutes, stirring occasionally, until the sauce thickens and begins to darken. Bottle quickly in sterilized jars and store in the refrigerator until required.

THIS CLASSIC SAUCE CAN BE
USED AS A CONDIMENT WITH ANY
MEAT DISH OR YOU CAN ALSO USE
IT TO MARINATE BEEF OR PORK
BEFORE GRILLING.

Homemade Ketchup

★ MAKES 1 CUP ★

PREP: 10 MINS

COOK: 15-20 MINS

INGREDIENTS

2 tablespoons olive oil

1 red onion, chopped

2 garlic cloves, chopped

4 plum or roma tomatoes, chopped

1 cup canned diced tomatoes

½ teaspoon ground ginger

½ teaspoon chili powder

⅓ cup firmly packed dark brown sugar

½ cup red wine vinegar

salt and pepper

1. Heat the olive oil in a large saucepan and add the onion, garlic, and all the tomatoes. Add the ginger and chili and season with salt and pepper. Cook for 15 minutes, or until soft.

2. Pour the mixture into a food processor or blender and blend well. Strain thoroughly to remove all the seeds. Return the mixture to the pan and add the sugar and vinegar. Return to a boil and cook until it is the consistency of ketchup.

3. Bottle quickly in sterilized jars and store in the refrigerator until required.

THIS HOMEMADE VERSION OF THE TRADITIONAL SAUCE IS MUCH MORE FLAVORSOME THAN STORE-BOUGHT KETCHUP.

Mayonnaise

 MAKES 1¼ CUPS

 PREP: 10 MINS

 COOK: NO COOKING

INGREDIENTS

2 extra-large egg yolks

2 teaspoons Dijon mustard

¾ teaspoon salt, or to taste

2 tablespoons lemon juice or white wine vinegar, plus extra if needed

about 1¼ cups sunflower oil

white pepper, to taste

1. Blend the egg yolks with the Dijon mustard, salt, and white pepper to taste in a food processor, blender, or by hand. Add the lemon juice and blend again.

2. With the motor still running, add the oil, drop by drop at first. When the sauce begins to thicken, the oil can then be added in a slow, steady stream. Taste and adjust the seasoning with extra salt, pepper, and lemon juice, if necessary. If the sauce seems too thick, slowly add 1 tablespoon of hot water or lemon juice.

3. Use immediately or store in a sterilized and airtight container in the refrigerator for up to 1 week.

THIS RICH AND CREAMY MAYONNAISE IS THE PERFECT ACCOMPANIMENT TO ANY BURGER OR SANDWICH.

Chipotle Ketchup &
Chipotle Mustard

 MAKES 1 CUP

 PREP: 10 MINS

 COOK: 3-10 MINS

INGREDIENTS

CHIPOTLE KETCHUP

1 cup ketchup

½ teaspoon
Worcestershire sauce

½ teaspoon packed
light brown sugar

1 tablespoon fresh lemon
juice, or to taste

1½ teaspoons chipotle
powder, or to taste

1 teaspoon ground cumin

½ teaspoon ground
turmeric

¼ teaspoon ground ginger

salt

CHIPOTLE MUSTARD

½ cup Dijon mustard

1 teaspoon chipotle
powder, or to taste

1. For the ketchup, combine all the ingredients in a small saucepan and put over medium heat. Bring to a simmer and cook, stirring frequently, for 5 minutes, or until the ketchup is slightly thickened. Remove from the heat and cool. Transfer to a sterilized jar, cover, and refrigerate until ready to use.

2. To make the chipotle mustard, put the ingredients in a small bowl and stir to thoroughly combine. Transfer to a sterilized jar, cover, and refrigerate until ready to use.

THESE SAUCES ARE GREAT FOR
ANY SPICE LOVERS WHO PREFER
THEIR BARBECUE RECIPES TO
HAVE A KICK TO THEM.

Roadhouse Steak Sauce

★ MAKES 1½ CUPS ★

PREP: 10 MINS

COOK: 50 MINS

INGREDIENTS

1 (14½-ounce) can diced tomatoes

⅔ cup beef stock or broth

4 garlic cloves, chopped

1 red onion, finely chopped

1 cup raisins

½ cup Worcestershire sauce

1 tablespoon beef extract or rich beef bouillon cube, crumbled

1 tablespoon dry mustard, dissolved in 1 tablespoon water

2 tablespoons white wine vinegar

1 tablespoon light corn syrup

1 tablespoon packed dark brown sugar

½ teaspoon cayenne pepper

finely grated zest of 1 orange

salt and pepper, to taste

1. Mix together all the ingredients in a heavy saucepan over high heat, stirring to dissolve the corn syrup and sugar. Bring to a boil, then reduce the heat to low and simmer, stirring freqently, for 30 minutes, or until the mixture is blended and the raisins are falling apart.

2. Transfer the mixture to a blender or food processor and puree. Strain the mixture through a fine-mesh strainer into the cleaned pan, rubbing back and forth with a wooden spoon and scraping the bottom of the strainer to produce as much puree as possible.

3. Put the pan over medium heat and bring the puree to a boil. Reduce the heat to medium-low and simmer, uncovered, for 15 minutes, or until the sauce has thickened and reduced. Transfer to a bowl and let cool completely. Adjust the salt and pepper, if necessary.

4. The sauce can be used immediately, or stored in a sterilized container in the refrigerator for up to 3 weeks.

Blistering Beer & Chili Sauce

INGREDIENTS

2 tablespoons sunflower oil

1 red onion, finely chopped

1 tablespoon ancho chili powder

1½ teaspoon cayenne pepper

1 cup ketchup

¼ cup molasses

2 tablespoons packed dark brown sugar

2 teaspoons salt

¼ teaspoon pepper

1⅓ cups pale ale

2 tablespoons apple cider vinegar or red wine vinegar

2 tablespoons Worcestershire sauce

3 red, green, or mixed jalapeño chiles, chopped

1. Heat the oil in a saucepan over medium-high heat. Add the onion and sauté for 3—5 minutes, or until soft. Add the chili powder and cayenne pepper, then stir for 30 seconds. Add the remaining ingredients, except the chiles, stirring until the ketchup, molasses, and sugar are blended.

2. Bring to a boil, skimming the surface, as necessary. Add the chiles. Reduce the heat and let gently simmer, skimming the surface as necessary and stirring occasionally, for about 30 minutes, or until the sauce has a coating consistency.

3. Transfer the sauce to a food processor or blender and puree. Pass the mixture through a fine-mesh strainer, rubbing back and forth with a wooden spoon and scraping the bottom of the strainer to produce as much puree as possible.

4. Use the sauce immediately or let it cool completely and store in a sterilized airtight container in the refrigerator for up to 2 weeks.

Celeriac, Fennel &
Peach Slaw

INGREDIENTS

¼ cup mayonnaise

1 teaspoon sriracha chili sauce

1 teaspoon horseradish sauce

juice and zest of 1 lemon

½ teaspoon pepper

2 ripe peaches, pitted and sliced

2½ cups julienned celeriac

1 fennel bulb, sliced

1 small red onion, sliced

1. In a large bowl, whisk together the mayonnaise, chili sauce, horseradish sauce, lemon zest, lemon juice, and pepper.

2. Add the peaches, celeriac, fennel, and onion to the bowl.

3. Mix well to combine thoroughly, then serve immediately.

THIS SLAW WILL WORK WELL
WITH ANY PITTED FRUIT AND
IS GREAT SERVED WITH PORK,
CHICKEN, OR FISH.

Creamy Potato Salad

SERVES 8

PREP: 15 MINS + CHILLING

COOK: 30 MINS

INGREDIENTS

2¾ pounds new potatoes

½ cup mayonnaise

¼ cup sour cream

⅓ cup white wine vinegar

1 teaspoon whole-grain mustard

½ teaspoon dried dill

½ cup finely chopped red onion

1 celery stalk, finely chopped

¼ cup chopped pickles

½ cup chopped roasted red pepper

2 hard-boiled eggs, chopped (optional)

salt and pepper, to taste

1. Put the unpeeled potatoes into a saucepan and cover with water by a few inches. Add salt, bring to a boil over high heat, then reduce the heat and simmer for 20—30 minutes, or until just tender.

2. Put the mayonnaise, sour cream, vinegar, mustard, dill, and salt and pepper into a bowl and mix together.

3. Drain the potatoes and let cool slightly, then slip off the skins with your fingers or with a paring knife. Chop the potatoes into ½-inch pieces and add to the dressing while still warm. Stir in the onion, celery, pickles, roasted pepper, and eggs, if using. Cover and chill for at least 2 hours or overnight.

THIS TRADITIONAL POTATO SALAD COMES WITH PICKLES, BELL PEPPERS, AND HARD-BOILED EGGS.

Smoky BBQ Beans

SERVES 4

PREP: 10 MINS

COOK: 30 MINS

INGREDIENTS

¼ cup olive oil

1 large onion, chopped

2 garlic cloves, chopped

2 celery stalks, chopped

1 large carrot, chopped

1 teaspoon fennel seeds

2 teaspoons
dried oregano

2 teaspoons
smoked paprika

1 tablespoon
chipotle paste

1 tablespoon molasses

2 cups tomato puree
or sauce

1 (15-ounce) can
cannellini beans,
drained and rinsed

salt and pepper,
to taste

1. Heat the oil in a large saucepan over medium heat. Add the onion, garlic, celery, and carrot and sauté, covered, for 15 minutes, or until translucent and softened.

2. Add the fennel seeds, oregano, paprika, chipotle, and molasses. Cook for 5 minutes to let the sugars start to caramelize.

3. Add the tomato puree and beans and cook for an additional 10 minutes.

4. Season and serve.

FOR THE MEAT-LOVING
CARNIVORE, TRY ADDING
SMOKED BACON OR CHORIZO.

Buttermilk Hamburger Buns

 ☆ MAKES 8-16 ☆

 PREP: 2½ HOURS

 COOK: 10-20 MINS

INGREDIENTS

3 cups white bread flour

1½ cups all-purpose flour, plus extra for dusting

1 stick butter, diced

1 extra-large egg

2 tablespoons sugar

2¼ teaspoons active dry yeast

1½ cups buttermilk

1 teaspoon salt

1 lightly beaten egg, to glaze

1. In a large bowl, mix together the flours and rub in the butter until it resembles fine bread crumbs.

2. In a medium bowl, whisk together the egg, sugar, yeast, buttermilk, and salt. Pour the egg mixture into the bowl with the flour. Using the back of a wooden spoon, combine all the ingredients together.

3. Tip the dough out onto a floured work surface and knead for 10 minutes, or until elastic and smooth. Put the dough into a clean bowl. Cover with plastic wrap and let rise in a warm place for 1½ hours.

4. Once the dough has risen, punch down with the palm of your hand, then turn out onto a floured surface. Divide the dough into 8 or 16, depending on whether you are making burger buns or slider rolls. Roll into ball shapes and put onto a large baking sheet, leaving enough space in between for the buns to double in size.

5. Cover the baking sheet with plastic wrap and let rise in a warm place for 30–40 minutes, or until doubled in size. Preheat the oven to 350°F.

6. Brush the buns lightly with the egg and bake in the preheated oven for 15–20 minutes for the large buns and 10–15 minutes for the smaller rolls.

MAKING BREAD BY HAND
IS A GREAT WAY OF
RELIEVING STRESS.

Corn on the Cob
with Blue Cheese

★ SERVES 6 ★

PREP: 20 MINS

COOK: 15-20 MINS

INGREDIENTS

1¼ cups crumbled blue cheese

⅔ cup cottage cheese

½ cup plain Greek yogurt

6 ears of corn

salt and pepper, to taste

1. Prepare the barbecue grill for direct cooking and preheat to medium. Put the blue cheese into a bowl. Beat with a wooden spoon until creamy. Beat in the cottage cheese until thoroughly blended. Gradually beat in the yogurt and season with salt and pepper. Cover with plastic wrap and let chill in a cool place until required.

2. Fold back the husks on each ear of corn and remove the silks. Smooth the husks back into place. Cut out six rectangles of double-thickness aluminum foil, each large enough to enclose an ear of corn. Wrap the corn in pieces of double-thickness aluminum foil.

3. Place the corn on the grill rack and cook for 15—20 minutes, turning frequently. Unwrap the corn and discard the foil. Peel back the husk on one side of each and trim off with a sharp knife. Transfer to serving plates and serve with the blue cheese mixture spooned on top.

IF YOU AREN'T A FAN OF
BLUE CHEESE, YOU COULD
REPLACE THIS WITH A SOFT
GOAT CHEESE INSTEAD.

Creamed Spinach

 SERVES 4

 PREP: 10 MINS

 COOK: 15-20 MINS

INGREDIENTS

½ cup olive oil

1 large shallot, diced

2 garlic cloves, crushed

4 ounces smoked bacon, chopped

1 large carrot, diced

2 cups diced celeriac

½ teaspoon salt

1 teaspoon pepper

1 cup heavy cream

1 (10-ounce) package fresh spinach

1. Heat the oil in a large saucepan over medium heat. Add the shallot, garlic, bacon, carrot, and celeriac. Sauté the vegetables, covered, for about 10 minutes, or until softened, stirring every now and then.

2. Season with the salt and pepper. Add the heavy cream and simmer the mixture until it is reduced by half.

3. Meanwhile, bring a medium saucepan of water to a boil. Blanch the spinach for a few seconds, then drain and run under cold water until the spinach is cooled. Squeeze out the excess water from the spinach, then add to the creamed vegetables. Stir to combine and serve immediately.

FOR A HEALTHIER VERSION, REPLACE THE HEAVY CREAM WITH LIGHT OR SOY CREAM.

Garlic Bread

SERVES 6

PREP: 15 MINS

COOK: 10-15 MINS

INGREDIENTS

1¼ sticks butter, softened

3 garlic cloves, crushed

2 tablespoons chopped fresh flat-leaf parsley

pepper, to taste

1 large or 2 small loaves of French bread

1. Prepare the barbecue grill for indirect cooking and preheat to medium-hot.

2. Mix the butter, garlic, and parsley together in a bowl until well combined. Season with pepper and mix well.

3. Make several lengthwise cuts in the bread but be careful not to cut all the way through.

4. Spread the flavored butter over one side of each cut and put the loaf onto a large sheet of double-thickness aluminum foil.

5. Wrap the bread in the foil, place on the grill rack, and cook for 10—15 minutes, or until the butter melts and the bread is piping hot. Serve immediately.

FOR AN ADDED TREAT, ADD SOME GRATED CHEESE TO THE CUTS IN THE BREAD AND COOK UNTIL MELTED.

Chapter 8
DRINKS

Fresh Lemonade

SERVES 6

PREP: 15 MINS
+ STANDING

COOK:
NO COOKING

INGREDIENTS

4 large lemons,
preferably unwaxed

¾ cup sugar

3¾ cups boiling water

ice cubes

1. Scrub the lemons well, then dry. Using a vegetable peeler, pare three of the lemons thinly. Put the peel into a heatproof bowl, add the sugar and boiling water, and stir well until the sugar has dissolved. Cover the bowl and let stand for at least 3 hours, stirring occasionally. Meanwhile, squeeze the juice from the three lemons and reserve.

2. Remove and discard the lemon peel and stir in the reserved lemon juice. Thinly slice the remaining lemon and cut the slices in half. Add to the lemonade along with the ice cubes. Stir and serve immediately.

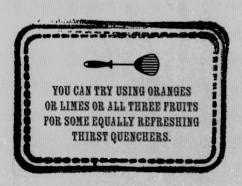

YOU CAN TRY USING ORANGES OR LIMES OR ALL THREE FRUITS FOR SOME EQUALLY REFRESHING THIRST QUENCHERS.

Tips for Hosting an Amazing BBQ

As summer days begin to heat up the air outside, you're probably starting to think about heating up the grill and inviting friends over to admire your grilling skills. With a little planning ahead, you can make it the event of the season.

1. Don't try to be a short-order cook. Keep the menu simple. Choose just three or four proteins at the most and do them well instead of trying to cook a million different things. Burgers (these can be hamburgers, turkey, fish, or veggie) or hot dogs, a beef dish, a chicken dish, and a fish or veggie dish are usually enough to satisfy most crowds. There's plenty of inspiration in this book for making these dishes as exciting and tasty as possible.

2. Do all of your prep ahead of time. Before a single flick of fire touches your grill, make sure you've chopped, sliced, marinated, and skewered everything you plan to put on the grill.

3. Put drinks on ice. Fill a large pail or cooler with ice and stock it with beer, soft drinks, and wine before your guests arrive. If you have a cohost who is willing to take charge of the drinks, offer homemade cocktails, punch, iced tea, etc. If you want to make fancy drinks, you can offer ice cubes with chunks of fruit or whole berries frozen in them.

4. Don't forget the condiments. For many, a hamburger's just not a burger if it's not dripping with sweet-salty-spicy sauces and loaded up with veggies. If you're serving hamburgers (or hot dogs) create a condiment station and set out an assortment of mustards, ketchups, relishes, pickled veggies, crunchy lettuce, sliced tomatoes, fresh herbs, chiles, and bacon and let guests choose their own accompaniments.

5. Serve make-ahead or store-bought appetizers. Don't make hungry guests stand around while you wait for the coals to get hot or that giant roast to cook through. Set out chips and salsa, assorted crudités with a bowl of creamy dip, or a cheese and cracker spread for people to nosh on while they take in your barbecuing prowess.

Sweet Iced Tea

SERVES 2

PREP: 15 MINS + CHILLING

COOK: 5 MINS

INGREDIENTS

1¼ cups water

2 tea bags

½ cup orange juice

¼ cup lime juice

1–2 tablespoons packed brown sugar

ice cubes

TO DECORATE

1 lime wedge

granulated sugar

orange or lime slices

1. Pour the water into a saucepan and bring to a boil. Remove from the heat, add the tea bags, and let steep for 5 minutes. Remove the tea bags and let the tea cool to room temperature. Transfer to a small bowl, cover with plastic wrap, and chill in the refrigerator for at least 45 minutes.

2. When the tea has chilled, pour in the orange juice and lime juice. Add sugar to taste.

3. Take two glasses and rub the rims with the lime wedge, then dip them in granulated sugar to frost. Put the ice cubes into the glasses and pour the tea over them. Decorate with orange or lime slices and serve immediately.

AT SUMMER PARTIES, PLACE PAILS FILLED WITH ICE CUBES AT VARIOUS POINTS SO GUESTS CAN HELP THEMSELVES.

Cookie Dough & Caramel
Cola Float

SERVES 4

PREP: 25 MINS
+ RESTING
+ FREEZING

COOK:
20 MINS

INGREDIENTS

COOKIE DOUGH ICE CREAM

4 tablespoons butter, softened

2 tablespoons packed light brown sugar

2 tablespoons packed dark brown sugar

2 teaspoons vanilla extract

⅔ cup all-purpose flour

⅓ cup semisweet chocolate chips

1 cup milk

6 egg yolks

¾ cup granulated sugar

1 cup heavy cream

⅔ cup caramel syrup

4 cups cola

1. In a food processor, beat together the butter and brown sugars for about 4 minutes, until pale. Add 1 teaspoon of the vanilla and the flour, then pulse until it starts to come together. Turn out onto a board and fold in the chocolate chips by hand.

2. Wrap the dough in plastic wrap and let rest in the refrigerator for 30 minutes.

3. Meanwhile, slowly heat the milk in a medium saucepan. In a heatproof bowl, whisk together the egg yolks, the remaining vanilla, and the granulated sugar. When the milk comes to a boil, remove from the heat and pour slowly into the egg mixture, whisking as you pour. Pour back into a clean saucepan and slowly heat, stirring with a wooden spoon. Do not let it boil. Remove from the heat when the sauce has thickened, then add the heavy cream and let cool slightly before putting into an ice cream machine. Churn until almost frozen.

4. Remove the cookie dough from the refrigerator and break it into walnut-size pieces. Add the pieces to the ice cream. Churn a couple of times to mix into the dough without breaking up the pieces too much. Transfer to a freezer container and freeze for an hour, or until required.

5. Scoop the ice cream into four tall glasses. Pour over the caramel, and top with cola.

IF YOU HAVE NOT GOT THE TIME
OR AN ICE CREAM MACHINE,
DON'T FEEL BAD ABOUT USING
STORE-BOUGHT ICE CREAM.

Spicy Bourbon Pickleback

INGREDIENTS

2 tablespoons bourbon

2 tablespoons liquid from a jalapeño pickle jar

1. Put the bourbon and pickle liquid in two separate shot glasses.

2. Knock back the bourbon.

3. Then drink the pickle juice in one shot as a chaser.

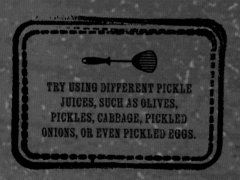

TRY USING DIFFERENT PICKLE JUICES, SUCH AS OLIVES, PICKLES, CABBAGE, PICKLED ONIONS, OR EVEN PICKLED EGGS.

Club Mojito

 SERVES 1

 PREP: 5 MINS

 COOK: NO COOKING

INGREDIENTS

1 teaspoon sugar syrup

6 fresh mint leaves, plus extra to decorate

juice of ½ lime

cracked ice

¼ cup Jamaican rum

club soda

dash Angostura bitters

1. Put the sugar syrup, mint leaves, and lime juice into a glass.

2. Muddle the mint leaves, then add cracked ice and the rum.

3. Fill up with club soda.

4. Finish with the Angostura bitters and decorate with the remaining mint leaves.

5. Serve immediately.

THIS FRESH AND FRUITY DRINK GOES DOWN WELL ON A HOT SUMMER'S DAY.

Red Wine Punch

SERVES 6

PREP: 10 MINS + MARINATING

COOK: NO COOKING

INGREDIENTS

juice of 1 orange

juice of 1 lemon

2 tablespoons confectioners' sugar

cracked ice

1 orange, thinly sliced

1 lemon, thinly sliced

1 bottle chilled red wine

lemon-lime soda, to taste

1. Put the orange juice and lemon juice into a bowl. Stir.

2. Add the sugar and stir. When the sugar has dissolved, add cracked ice.

3. Add the sliced fruit and the wine and marinate for 1 hour.

4. Add lemon-lime soda to taste, then fill up with cracked ice.

5. Serve immediately.

THIS IS A GREAT COCKTAIL TO SERVE WHEN GUESTS ARRIVE AT THE BARBECUE.

Whiskey Sling

PREP: 5 MINS

COOK: NO COOKING

INGREDIENTS

1 teaspoon confectioners' sugar

2 tablespoons lemon juice

1 teaspoon water

¼ cup blended whiskey

cracked ice

1 orange wedge

1. Put the sugar into a glass.

2. Add the lemon juice and water and stir until the sugar has dissolved.

3. Pour in the whiskey and stir to mix.

4. Fill a small, chilled glass halfway with cracked ice and strain the cocktail over it. Decorate with the orange wedge.

5. Serve immediately.

THIS IS AN IDEAL END OF THE NIGHT COCKTAIL FOR ALL WHISKEY LOVERS.

Beer Cocktail

☆ SERVES 2 ☆

PREP: 5 MINS

COOK: NO COOKING

INGREDIENTS

2 tablespoons port

⅔ cup stout

1 cup ginger beer or ginger ale

dash of orange Angostura bitters

ice cubes

1. Pour the port, stout, ginger beer, and bitters into a cocktail shaker.

2. Top with ice cubes, put the lid on, and shake the cocktail vigorously.

3. Pour the drink over ice in two glasses and serve.

THIS RECIPE MAKES A GREAT PUNCH. JUST INCREASE THE QUANTITIES AND ADD A FEW ORANGE SLICES.

Salty Dog

SERVES 1   PREP: 5 MINS   COOK: NO COOKING

INGREDIENTS

1 tablespoon sugar

1 tablespoon coarse salt

1 lime wedge

cracked ice

¼ cup vodka

grapefruit juice, to taste

1. Mix the sugar and salt in a saucer.

2. Rub the rim of a chilled cocktail glass with the lime wedge.

3. Dip into the sugar and salt mixture, to coat.

4. Fill the glass with cracked ice and pour the vodka over it. Fill up with the grapefruit juice and stir.

5. Serve immediately.

THE SHARP FLAVORS OF THE GRAPEFRUIT JUICE AND VODKA COMBINE BEAUTIFULLY WITH THE SUGAR AND SALT.

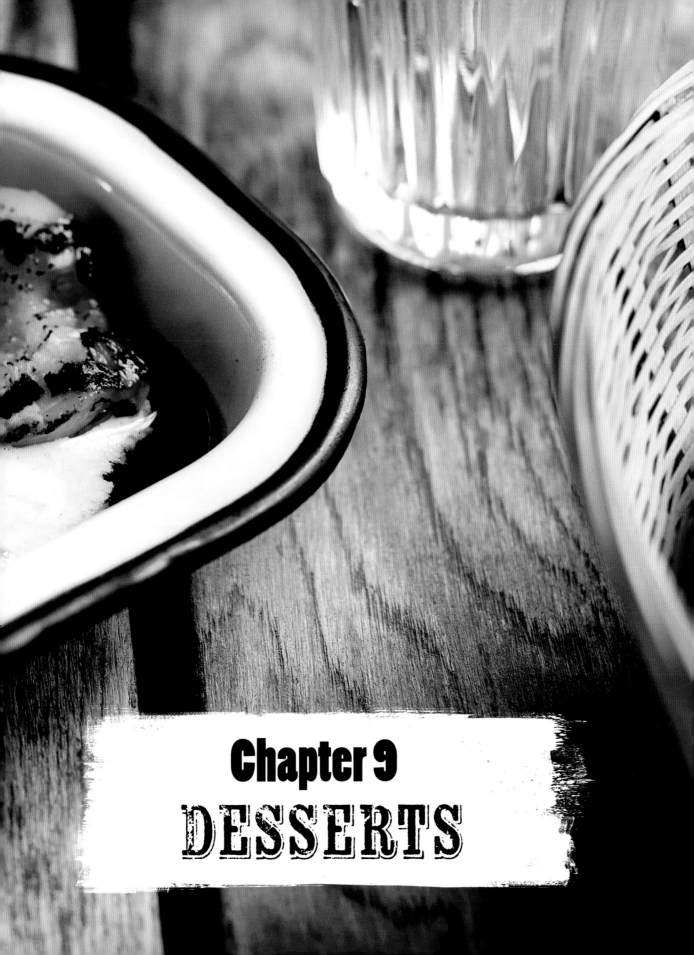

Chapter 9
DESSERTS

Grilled Bourbon Peaches

 SERVES 4

 PREP: 15 MINS

 COOK: 20 MINS

INGREDIENTS

6 ripe peaches, pitted and halved

1 tablespoon oil

¼ cup good-quality bourbon

1 stick butter

⅔ cup firmly packed dark brown sugar

1 teaspoon vanilla extract

⅔ cup apple juice

vanilla ice cream, to serve

1. Prepare the barbecue grill for direct cooking and preheat to hot.

2. Brush the flesh side of the peach halves with the oil.

3. In a saucepan over high heat, flambé the bourbon, then add the butter, sugar, vanilla, and apple juice. Bring to a simmer and let everything dissolve and turn slightly syrupy. Remove from the heat and let cool.

4. Lay the peaches, skin side down, on the grill rack and cook for 2 minutes, or until the skins starts to char. Carefully turn over with a spatula and cook for an additional 2 minutes.

5. Remove the peaches from the grill and serve with ice cream and the bourbon syrup.

TRY THIS RECIPE WITH
A MIXTURE OF PITTED FRUIT
AND USE RUM INSTEAD
OF BOURBON.

Chocolate & Rum Bananas

SERVES 4   PREP: 15 MINS   COOK: 5-10 MINS

INGREDIENTS

1 tablespoon butter, melted

8 ounces semisweet or milk chocolate

4 large bananas

2 tablespoons rum

mascarpone cheese, to serve

1. Prepare the barbecue grill for direct cooking and preheat to medium. Take four large squares of double-thickness aluminum foil and brush them with the butter.

2. Cut the chocolate into small pieces. Carefully make a slit, lengthwise, in the peel of each banana, and open just wide enough to insert the chocolate. Place the chocolate pieces inside the bananas, along their lengths, then close them up.

3. Wrap each stuffed banana in a square of foil. Place on the grill rack and cook for 5—10 minutes, or until the chocolate has melted. Remove from the heat, place the bananas on plates, and pour some rum into each banana.

4. Serve immediately with mascarpone cheese.

FOR CHILDREN, SIMPLY OMIT
THE RUM AND INSTEAD SERVE
WITH MARSHMALLOWS AND
ICE CREAM.

Choosing the Right Smoking Wood

MILD

For mild smoke flavor, choose alder or fruit woods, such as apple or cherry. They'll impart a mild smokiness with a hint of fruity sweetness. These are great choices for smoking more delicate foods, such as poultry or fish. Alder is especially mild with a hint of sweetness. Apple and cherry offer fruity notes and go well with either chicken or pork.

MEDIUM

For a medium smoke flavor, oak, hickory, or maple are your best bets. They'll impart a distinctive and intense smokiness without overpowering the meat. These are great choices for poultry, pork, or beef. Hickory is probably the most common smoking wood. Its flavor is intense, so it is often mixed with a milder wood to tone it down. Oak offers a milder smokiness than hickory and a little more flavor than apple or cherry, making it a good wood to mix with hickory.

HEAVY

Mesquite, the smokiest of all the smoking woods, is what is typically used for a Texas-style barbecue. That's because hearty meats, such as brisket, can hold their own against the intense smoke flavor it delivers. Used sparingly, in combination with milder woods, it can be used successfully for fish, chicken, pork, or beef.

Banana & Chocolate
S'mores

 SERVES 4

 PREP: 15 MINS

 COOK: 10-15 MINS

INGREDIENTS

8 marshmallows

8 chocolate chip cookies

1 banana, thinly sliced

4 squares semisweet chocolate

1. Prepare the barbecue grill for direct cooking and preheat to medium.

2. Thread two of the marshmallows onto presoaked wooden skewers or metal skewers. Toast over the grill until they soften.

3. Place the toasted marshmallows on top of a cookie, top with a few slices of banana and a square of chocolate, and sandwich together with another cookie. Repeat with the remaining cookies, marshmallows, and other ingredients. Serve each s'more while they are still hot.

THIS IS A TWIST ON THE CLASSIC CAMPFIRE DESSERT OF S'MORES. THIS VERSION USES CHOCOLATE CHIP COOKIES.

Boozy Nectarines

 **SERVES 4**

 PREP: 15 MINS

 **COOK: 15-20 MINS**

INGREDIENTS

8 ripe nectarines

4 tablespoons butter,
plus extra for greasing

3 tablespoons
raw brown sugar

amaretto liqueur

vanilla ice cream,
to serve

1. Prepare the barbecue grill for direct cooking and preheat to medium-low. Brush eight pieces of double-thickness aluminum foil with butter.

2. Place a nectarine on each square of foil. Top with a small pat of butter, a sprinkle of sugar, and a few drops of the amaretto liqueur. Wrap the foil into a loose package, sealing well.

3. Place on the grill rack and cook, with the lid on, for 15—20 minutes, or until tender. Serve immediately with ice cream.

THESE BOOZY NECTARINES
ALSO WORK WELL WITH COGNAC
OR BRANDY.

Fruit Skewers

 SERVES 4

 PREP: 15 MINS

 COOK: 5-10 MINS

INGREDIENTS

a selection of fruit, such as apricots, peaches, strawberries, mangoes, pineapple, and bananas, prepared and cut into chunks

2 tablespoons maple syrup, plus extra for drizzling

2 ounces semisweet chocolate (optional)

1. Prepare the barbecue grill for direct cooking and preheat to medium-hot.

2. Thread alternate pieces of fruit onto four presoaked wooden skewers or metal skewers. Brush the fruit with the maple syrup.

3. Put the chocolate, if using, into a heatproof bowl. Set the bowl over a saucepan of barely simmering water and stir until the chocolate has completely melted.

4. Place the skewers on the grill rack and cook for 3 minutes, or until caramelized. Transfer to serving plates and serve immediately, drizzled with the melted chocolate, if using, and maple syrup.

THESE SKEWERS COULD ALSO
BE SERVED WITH LOW-FAT
FROMAGE BLANC OR GREEK
YOGURT INSTEAD OF THE
MELTED CHOCOLATE.

Caramelized Apple Slices

 SERVES 4

 PREP: 15 MINS

 COOK: 5–6 MINS

INGREDIENTS

4 crisp sweet apples, such as Braeburn

juice of ½ lemon

3 tablespoons raw brown sugar

¼ teaspoon ground cinnamon

2 tablespoons butter, melted, plus extra for oiling

vanilla ice cream or whipped cream, to serve

1. Prepare the barbecue grill for direct cooking and preheat to hot.

2. Remove and discard a thin slice from the top and bottom of the apples. Remove the cores and slice each apple into three thick rings. Put into a bowl and toss with the lemon juice to prevent discoloration.

3. Mix the sugar and cinnamon and sprinkle the mix over the apples, tossing thoroughly to coat. Brush with some of the melted butter. Reserve any liquid in a bowl.

4. Brush the grill rack with butter. Place the apples on the grill rack and cook for 5—6 minutes, or until golden and slightly charred, turning every 2 minutes and brushing with butter and the reserved liquid. Transfer to serving bowls and serve immediately with ice cream.

INDEX

INDEX